WILD FLOWERS

WILD FLOWERS

Country Classics for the Contemporary Garden

ROB PROCTOR

PHOTOGRAPHY BY ROB GRAY

WATERCOLOURS AND SUPPLEMENTAL
PHOTOGRAPHS BY THE AUTHOR

FOREWORD BY MIRIAM ROTHSCHILD

CASSELL

FOR ANGELA

The best of teachers
and the best of friends.

Cassell Publishers Limited
Villiers House
41/47 Strand
London WC2N 5JE

Copyright © Running Heads Incorporated 1991

All rights reserved. This book is protected by copyright. No part of it may be reproduced, stored in a retrieval system, transmitted in any form or by any means, electronic, mechanical, photocopying, recording or otherwise, without written permission from the publishers.

First published in Great Britain in 1991

A RUNNING HEADS BOOK

British Library Cataloguing in Publication Data

Proctor, Rob
   Antique flowers : wild flowers
   1. Gardens. Ornamental wild flowering plants. Cultivation.
   I. Title
   635.9676

   ISBN 0-304-34043-X

WILD FLOWERS was conceived and produced by
Running Heads Incorporated
55 West 21 Street
New York, NY 10010

Editor: Charles A. de Kay
Designer: Jan Melchior
Managing Editor: Lindsey Crittenden
Production Manager: Linda Winters

Typeset by Trufont Typographers, Inc.
Colour separations by Hong Kong Scanner Craft Co., Ltd.
Printed and bound in Singapore by Times Offset Pte. Ltd.

Gardeners have long held a special affection for the wildflowers of their own region, as well as for those from around the world. Rob Gray's photographs capture these flowers growing in lovely gardens on both sides of the Atlantic. We extend our thanks to the generous people who opened their homes and gardens to us.

Ruth Koch
Michael and Kate Eagleton
Sandy Snyder
Anne Weckbaugh
Tweet Kimball
Betsy Herrick
Beth Chatto
Tom Peace
Pat Pachuta
The Honorable Governor of Colorado
   and Mrs. Roy Romer
Diana Monday
Margaret Fuller
Ken and Betty Lou Roberts
Karen and Jim Esquibel
Mary Kay Long and Dennis Unites
Elfreda Sacarto
Nancy Stimson Watters
The Cloisters
Denver Botanic Gardens

Garden in the Woods
Arnold Arboretum
The Molly Brown House
Blackberry River Inn
Hidcote Manor Garden
Sissinghurst Castle Garden
Cambridge University Botanic Garden
Old Sturbridge Village
Dyffryn Gardens

Special thanks to:

Lauren Springer
Deane Hall
Robert Heapes
Robin Preston
Angela Overy
Panayoti Kelaidis
Ray Daugherty

Solange Gignac and Ellen Mackey
   of The Helen Fowler Library,
   Denver Botanic Gardens
Diane Dalton
Nancy Ballek MacKinnon,
   Ballek's Garden Center
Mary and Procter Naylor
Jeanne Ruggles
Starr Tapp
Kathy Meyer
Lianne Meyer
Judy Holland
Mary Hart
Susan Sheridan
Lin Hulbert
Bea Taplin
David Macke
Edward Connors
Annie Duncan
Andrew Pierce

CONTENTS

FOREWORD • 9

INTRODUCTION

Foreigners Welcome Here • 11

CHAPTER ONE

Conquest and Cultivation • 21

CHAPTER TWO

Green Cargoes • 33

CHAPTER THREE

A Garden from the Wilderness • 41

CHAPTER FOUR
A Portfolio of Antique Species ◆ 53

Anemone canadensis Canadian Anemone
Anemone × hybrida Japanese Windflower
Anemone sylvestris Snowdrop Windflower
Anemone virginiana Thimbleweed
Aquilegia caerulea Rocky Mountain Columbine
Aquilegia canadensis Canadian Columbine
Aquilegia formosa Jester's Cap
Aquilegia vulgaris Granny Bonnets
Armeria maritima Sea Pink
Asclepias tuberosa Butterfly Weed
Aster divaricatus White Wood Aster
Aster novae-angliae Michaelmas Daisy
Aster novi-belgii New York Aster
Callirhoe involucrata Wine Cup
Chelone obliqua Turtle-head
Chrysanthemum balsamita Costmary
Chrysanthemum leucanthemum Ox-eye Daisy
Chrysanthemum parthenium Feverfew
Cimicifuga racemosa Black Snakeroot
Coreopsis lanceolata Tickseed
Coreopsis tinctoria Calliopsis
Coreopsis verticillata Thread-leaf Coreopsis
Daucus carota Queen Anne's Lace
Echinacea purpurea Purple Coneflower
Epilobium angustifolium Willow Herb
Eupatorium purpureum Joe Pye Weed
Eupatorium rugosum White Snakeroot
Gaillardia aristata Firewheel
Gaillardia pulchella Indian Blanket
Gaura lindheimeri Apple-blossom Grass
Gentiana clausa Closed Gentian
Gillenia trifoliata Bowman's Root
Glaucium flavum Horned Poppy
Helenium autumnale Sneezeweed
Heuchera americana Alum Root

Heuchera sanguinea Coralbells
Ipomopsis aggregata Skyrocket
Ipomopsis rubra Standing Cypress
Lathyrus latifolius Everlasting Pea
Liatris pycnostachya Button Snakeroot
Liatris spicata Gayfeather
Lilium canadense Meadow Lily
Lilium philadelphicum Wood Lily
Lilium superbum Turk's-cap Lily
Lilium tigrinum Tiger Lily
Lobelia cardinalis Cardinal Flower
Lobelia siphilitica Great Lobelia

Mentzelia laevicaulis Blazing Star
Mentzelia lindleyi California Star
Monarda citriodora Lemon Mint
Monarda didyma Bee Balm
Monarda punctata Horsemint
Oenothera biennis Evening Primrose
Oenothera caespitosa Matted Evening Primrose
Oenothera fruticosa Sundrop
Oenothera speciosa White Evening Primrose
Papaver nudicaule Iceland Poppy
Papaver rhoeas Flanders Poppy
Penstemon barbatus Scarlet Bugler
Penstemon pinifolius Prairie Fire
Penstemon strictus Rocky Mountain Penstemon
Physostegia formosior False Dragon Head
Physostegia virginiana Obedience
Ratibida columnifera Mexican Hat
Rudbeckia hirta Black-eyed Susan
Rudbeckia laciniata Green-headed Coneflower
Rudbeckia triloba Brown-eyed Susan
Saponaria officinalis Soapwort
Sidalcea malviflora Checkerbloom
Solidago canadensis Canada Goldenrod
Solidago sempervirens Seaside Goldenrod
Symphytum officinale Comfrey
Vernonia noveboracensis Ironweed
Zauschneria arizonica Hummingbird's Trumpet
Zauschneria californica California Fuchsia

Sources ◆ 145

Where to Find the Flowers ◆ 146
Nurseries and Seed Merchants ◆ 150
Table of Conversions ◆ 153

Bibliography ◆ 155

Index ◆ 157

THIS IS A DELIGHTFUL BOOK. The author tells us it's about wild and naturalized flowers, but it has infinitely wider horizons than this title suggests. The early chapters introduce us to the ancient white lily used by Roman foot soldiers to treat their corns and bunions—the same Madonna Lily which bursts into bloom at dawn on Easter Sunday and which suddenly gave forth an exquisite fragrance when touched by Mary. . . .

The volume then sweeps on through delicious Greek myths to the Dark Ages, the Crusades, the Babylonians, the Egyptians, the Persians, with passing glimpses of Nebuchadnezzar, Achilles, Hercules, St. Veronica, and Linnaeus. Furthermore, we are whisked through the United States, from California and Washington to Texas, and from the United Kingdom to Japan, Italy, France and China. It opens up a wonderful vista of garlanded landscapes with a hint of divine inspiration and the poetic beauty of wild flowers.

I am glad the author draws attention to the fact that every garden flower was once wild somewhere. . . . Perhaps this is why I like mixing cultivated varieties with local wild plants. I grow the 'Étoile d'Hollande' —one of the greatest creations of man— up the walls of my house with 'Iceberg' rioting on the left side and the Dog Rose on the right. They complement one another. Secretly, I am hooked on the Dog Rose—a blissfully untidy plant with wild grace, distilling the essence of June sunshine.

I cannot, however, completely agree

FOREWORD BY MIRIAM ROTHSCHILD

with Rob Proctor when he writes, "Country flowers by and large take care of themselves." They certainly do in nature, though competition is keen, but moved into a kitchen garden or grown in a herbaceous border they require careful "nannying." In the early days I decided to grow Cowslips in rows in big squares, like cabbages, with the object of ultimately collecting seed. After an initial burst of unusually vigorous growth, they seemed to contract every disease known to horticulturists and some besides. Of course, this is not surprising because we really know very little indeed about wild flowers, for they have not been studied and selected for cultivation for hundreds of years like the horticultural plants we purchase in garden centres.

This is why this particular volume is so immensely useful, for the author has collected such diverse and scattered facts about the individual species he describes— not only their history but their habits, cultivation, preferences, and distribution. I was also delighted by the variety and charm of the common names of the plants from the United States, many of which are new to me: Blazing Star, Bee Balm, Bouncing Bet, Hummingbird's Trumpet, and so forth.

In addition to its botanical and horticultural information, this book might also serve as a bare-foot doctor's handbook! It is full of old wives' tales of medicinal cures and miraculous remedies. One could wish for some information about modern research into these matters. Curiosity is aroused, for instance, by the fact that Comfrey (in various languages) is designated a bone-healing plant. Has any laboratory looked into this claim? I myself have shown that one of its toxic alkaloids is sequestered and stored as a protective device by the brilliant Scarlet Tiger Moth. I wish I had had this book at that moment in time! Similarly, I was ignorant of the fact that the Butterfly Weed (*Asclepias tuberosa*) was used for medicinal purposes in days gone by in North America. Again I came across this group of plants when I was researching the storage of heart poisons—akin to digitalis—by the Monarch Butterfly. The caterpillar of this insect feeds on the leaves of Asclepias and, as Rob Proctor points out, the imagoes flock to collect the nectar of the "most beautiful wild flower".

The book is packed with delectable information and will appeal to a large audience on both sides of the Atlantic.

INTRODUCTION

FOREIGNERS WELCOME HERE

The pleasure that is received from it is for a man (whom the ignorant think to be alone) to have plants speaking Greek and Latin to him, and putting him in mind of stories which otherwise he would never think of.

William Cole
The Art of Simpling (1657)

EVERY GARDEN FLOWER WAS once wild, plucked from the meadow or the woods. Many of these country flowers have been tamed over the course of history. Methodical Greeks studied the plants of their empire carefully to discover their uses. Their knowledge was passed down to medieval monks, who planted flowers for the healing arts and the stew pot within their cloistered gardens. These "simples" arrived in North America with the colonists. Native Americans found a medicinal or culinary use for nearly every plant around them, and their uses of country flowers mingled with the folk medicine from the Old World. Tradition and superstition from around the world spice the melting pot of horticulture. The mystique of wildflowers, even tame ones, continues to intrigue us.

In every culture, myth and legend explained the presence on earth of wild flowers of the countryside. The Greeks were masters at myth, and no place on earth could compete with the floral miracles transpiring on the storied hill of Parnassus, overlooking Delphi, where Apollo spoke through his oracle. Many of our garden flowers sprang to life on that hill, like the narcissus, transformed from the body of a vain fellow who wept himself to death for love of his own image. White roses grew on the hillside; they pricked Venus with their thorns as she ran to the dying Adonis, and so turned red from shame. The Adonis flower took his name and its crimson colour from his blood, and Venus's tears became anemones.

In Greek mythology it seems sudden conversion from goddess or nymph to flower was an everyday occurrence on Par-

nassus. Syrinx, chased by Pan, was rescued from his unwelcome advances by becoming *Syringa*, the lilac, or, in some versions, a mock orange. Pan was the musically inclined god of pastures and flocks (symbolized by his goat-like horns). It was said he fashioned his pipe from the stem of the shrub traditionally used in pipe-making. So it seems the poor Syrinx could not escape his lips even through transmutation. Diana similarly saved a nymph, presumably Viola, from the embraces of her brother Apollo by turning her into the violet (apparently a fate preferable to life on Olympus). Apollo further diminished the ranks of the immortals when the nymph Daphne opted for transfiguration into a sweet-smelling shrub rather than put up with his pursuit. Mortals wandered the fabled hill as well; King Lysimachus plucked a stem of yellow loosestrife, *Lysimachia*, to halt a charging bull. Here grew parsley, chosen by Hercules for his first garland, and mullein, burned as torches at funerals and gathered by witches for incantations.

For centuries flowers held potent magical powers. Rue, *Ruta graveolens*, protected the ancients from the evil eye. The "herb of grace," as it was later dubbed by Shakespeare, also had the power to keep a maiden from going wrong in affairs of the heart, if only she would have the sense (or inclination) to nibble a leaf before she was swept off her feet. The common sage, *Salvia officinalis*, could be similarly employed, allowing girls to see their future husbands. Sage kept off toads as well, perhaps benefitting countless medieval wartless brides.

Flowers were the province of fairies in folktales. Whereas Greek myths represented the awesome and often brutal forces of nature, English and Northern European fairy stories reflected a gentler, more whimsical outlook. The little people took shelter in anemones, the silken petals enfolding them at night. They hid in the cups of primroses by day, and it was said that a person who believed could hear a high, sweet song emanating from the flowers like the harmonized hum of a bee. (Never mind that it could be an extraordi-

Antique flowers thrive at the Cloisters in New York City, LEFT. *Epilobium angustifolium*, ABOVE, blooms in early summer.

narily gifted bee.) The flowers of St.-John's-wort were believed to be daylight disguises of fairy horses. Should an unwary soul tread on them after sunset, a horse would arise and gallop off with the unwilling passenger, leaving him at daybreak far from home. This was likely a widely used excuse by drunken husbands in medieval days. Not all flower lore was as benign. English children have long believed that if they picked the flowers of *Lychnis flos-cuculi*, they would be struck by lightning—all the more amazing, since such consequences were usually reserved for poisonous plants.

During the Dark Ages, monks kept the knowledge of the Greeks and Romans alive as the barbarians swept over Europe. The secret healing powers were passed down, and like a story told time and again, embellishments and distortions occurred. Christian doctrine likewise coloured or transformed the works of the ancients. *Lilium candidum*, the ancient white lily used by Roman foot soldiers to treat corns and bunions, was borne by the angel of the Annunciation. Mary touched the flower, which to that point had been scentless, and it gave forth an exquisite fragrance. The Madonna Lily was said to burst forth into bloom on Easter dawn.

On her way to Bethlehem, the Virgin stopped to rest and hung her cloak on a bush. When she removed it, the shrub called Rosemary burst into bloom and also bore a sweet scent. A similar transformation altered another flower. Saint Veronica wiped the blood and sweat from Christ's face on the way to Calvary. The cloth bore his miraculous portrait, a *vera ikonika*, a true image, whence *Veronica*. The blood fell on the flowers she was wearing, causing

Lychnis flos-cuculi, ABOVE, dots marshes. The genus *Heracleum*, BELOW, honours Hercules. Everlasting Pea, Rue, and Wallflower circle Madonna Lily, RIGHT.

them to become holy and bear her name. The legend is confusing, in that it is unclear which came first, the name of the saint or the miracle.

Ornithogalum, the little bulb we call Star of Bethlehem, came from the Middle East, where it is roasted and eaten. Legend told how it had once been a part of the light that shone above the stable where Christ was born. Having led the wise men and shepherds to their destination, the star burst like a meteor, scattering its flowers.

The Turks set into motion an extraordinary phenomenon in 1453 by capturing Constantinople, forcing many Greek scholars to flee to Italy. The influx aroused a new interest in the classics and learning in general. By the next century, the effect of this renaissance had spread throughout the continent. The fledgling science of botany emerged as the long-forgotten texts of the Greeks and Romans came to light. It was fortunate that Carolus Linnaeus was there to chart its course. He simplified the tangle of Latin and medieval muddle used to name plants into the two-word genus and species format we use today. Initial resistance to the system he first proposed in 1737 (imagine classifying plants by their methods of sexual reproduction, scorned the critics) faded in time. Linnaeus revered the ancient scholarly writings of the Greeks and Romans, and incorporated the names of plants they had used. In addition, he fancied mythology, and encouraged the use of the names of legendary figures to name the flowers of antiquity. Thus, the poetry of mythology was preserved in the names of *Achillea*, named for Achilles, *Tithonia*, after fickle Aurora's mortal beau Tithonius, and *Heracleum*, for mighty Hercules.

Legend clings to Star-of-Bethlehem, BELOW.
Aster divaricatus blooms in a woodland clearing, RIGHT.

The marks and colours that inspired fables long ago are still impressed on the leaves and petals, and the symbolism is deeply engrained in our culture. We still speak of laurelled brows, willowy grace, the lily of purity, the oak of strength, and palms of victory; we extend the olive branch of peace (after, perhaps, pointing out the prune of face). In our comparatively dull age, flowers continue to perpetuate the poetry and mystery with which our ancestors used to explain them when the world was young.

Wherever they thrive, some flowers have come to symbolize a region and the people who live there. Bougainvillea drapes the walls of New Orleans homes; roses glow on every street in Portland. Bluebonnets signify Texas; sunflowers are synonymous with Kansas. Heathers evoke images of Scotland, bluebells of English woods. The beloved yellow cowslip perfectly represents the magical peace of English fields and hedgerows. Washington, D.C. is known for its cherry trees, a gift early in this century from the city of Tokyo.

When flowers have been introduced to new lands, they sometimes become a part of the natural landscape. This book is about the wild and naturalized flowers— the country flowers—that have become enduring symbols in particular places where they grow abundantly. There is no strict definition for a country flower: it is one that thrives on its own either in the field or forest, but may grace the garden as well. They might best be described as "charming" or "old-fashioned" and are steeped in the lore and legend of their homelands. Most of them may be successfully grown, with their mysteries in-

tact, by gardeners throughout North America and Europe. Country flowers include annuals, which grow, flower, and die in a single season, and perennials, which are winter hardy, returning to bloom for many years. A few are biennial, taking two years to complete their cycle.

In some areas, a few of these country flowers may be characterized by the uncharitable as weeds. I do not fall back on

the hackneyed axiom about a weed being a flower that is growing in the wrong place (though I occasionally agree that some weeds are merely plants we have not yet learned to appreciate). There are genuine weeds with unredeeming virtues, but only climate and the gardener's temperament can make the distinction between "exuberant," "invasive," and "insidious."

Each gardener fights a battle with a plant or two. When I think of hell, I envision the path leading there paved not with good intentions, but with Puncture Vine. I struggle to conquer this *Tribulus terrestris* (the name means, literally, "terror of the earth"), a creeper originally from Africa with thorny seed pods capable of piercing bicycle tyres, dogs' paws, and unwary barefooted gardeners. My neighbour, a professor of theology, espouses the theory that the seeds are sown at night by the devil himself, and I would not presume to argue with such a learned man. The plant has invaded vast areas of the southwestern United States, and has staked a (disputed) claim to my garden.

I am overrun by exuberant California Poppies and Bachelor's Buttons, but that is by choice. Dill, Perilla, and Cosmos expand their colonies, too, but I'm inclined to think that too much of a good thing is wonderful. Every gardener, however, has an individual standard to measure wonderfulness, and so must decide which country flowers to admit to the garden.

Country flowers, by and large, take care of themselves, though not all of them will thrive in every garden in every region. Rainfall, soil type, and temperature extremes must be taken into account, though few true gardeners are daunted by such considerations. Gardeners in arid lands coax roses to bloom, and those in rainy regions find ways to enjoy the prickly pleasures of cactus. Gardeners can grow flowers from around the globe by one means or another. Travelling is not necessary to procure souvenirs from exotic lands, since so many flowers arrived hundreds of years ago for extended trips. Many gardeners, of course, love to travel. It is a rare one who does not return from a foreign land without a slip of a plant tucked in the toe of a shoe, though we mustn't condone these customs violations.

It is the rare gardener, too, who does not harbour a stowaway flower from the past. Some have become such a part of the natural landscape, or such a respectable member of the border, that their pasts have been forgotten. Country flowers rode with the Crusaders, crossed on the May-

flower, and travelled by wagon train to the California gold fields. Country flowers discovered in the New World sailed to Europe, where they were received by royalty and introduced to high society. Although their fortunes rose and fell on the currencies of fashion, these antique plants are with us still. Learning their stories is part of the pleasure of growing them, as they return to beds and borders in town and country gardens everywhere.

Heuchera sanguinea, FAR LEFT, is a cottage garden classic. Ox-eye Daisy, LEFT, spread from southern Europe. *Aquilegia formosa*, ABOVE, is indigenous to the Pacific Northwest.

CHAPTER ONE

CONQUEST AND CULTIVATION

There is not a softer trait to be found in the character of those stern men than that they should have been sensible of these flower-roots clinging among the fibres of their rugged hearts, and felt the necessity of bringing them over sea, and making them hereditary in the new land.

Nathaniel Hawthorne
American Notebooks

FLOWERS HAVE LONG BEEN grown for their beauty alone. The Babylonians, Egyptians, and Persians cultivated ornamental gardens, at considerable expenditure of their resources, featuring what their desert lands did not naturally possess: abundant water and exotic flowers. When King Nebuchadnezzar built the Hanging Gardens of Babylon in the sixth century B.C. for his wife, he raised horticultural standards to new heights, namely to seven stories. A special well stored water from which leather buckets were raised to the upper tiers. The gardens covered three acres and, from a distance, were said to resemble a green mountain—most unusual and awe-inspiring floating above the desert sands. The more conventional and less ostentatious Persian garden, a geometric design of reflecting pools and shafts of cypress trees, studded with tubs of flowering plants, was adapted by the Greeks. They enclosed it within the walls of house—a garden court open to the sky.

Ideas that seem to have sprung from the golden age of gardening in seventeenth- and eighteenth-century England actually came from the golden age of Rome. It is in the writings of Pliny the Younger that we first find a consideration of the view of wild country from within the confines of an orderly garden. His garden design considered vistas that were to be viewed from every angle as highbrow guests moved about, deep in philosophical conversation. Pliny and his guests dined seated around a marble pool, floating plates back and forth across the surface. This innovation never seems to have caught on, perhaps due to too many capsized entrées. The Romans also coaxed roses into bloom in winter by planting them near hot water pipes; it would be two thousand years before the inventors of the greenhouse would capitalize on this idea.

The formality of Greek and Roman gardens would blossom again in Italy during the Renaissance. The orderly and ornate terraces of the Italianate style brought or-

Wildflowers fill the meadow at the Arnold Arboretum, ABOVE. Lupins frame a pastoral view, RIGHT.

der, symbolically, out of the vestiges of the past, as well as from the rough countryside. Formal gardens owe much to their origins in hot, sunny climates, where the shade, provided by their enclosure, was so appreciated. The classical bent of the Italians would ripple throughout the Continent, causing the greatest stir in France.

MONTEZUMA'S REVENGE

Influences, other than western ones, shaped gardens to come. The horticultural traditions of the Chinese evolved over thousands of years, though these sensibilities were not to make an impact on Western culture until long after many of the plants they grew had been introduced. The asymmetrical Chinese gardens—tranquil enclosures where proportion and scale were carefully manipulated to suggest a vast natural world—would be widely mimicked by Westerners but never completely understood. The influence of the Orient, however, encouraged a break with formal rigidity in Europe. A vogue for incongruous garden ornament, perhaps best demonstrated by the pagoda at Kew Gardens, was the first giddy trend, though the English landscape school was the indirect result. But I'm getting ahead of myself.

The floating gardens of the Aztecs were a marvel of horticultural ingenuity. Flowers, vegetables, and fruits were grown on rafts in the shallow lake of Xochimilco. Native American gardening traditions died a quick and agonizing death as the empires were torn asunder by Spanish conquests. The gardens were laid to waste, but the plants eventually made their way to Europe. Nasturtiums, zinnias, dahlias, and amaranths would ultimately fuel the fires of the carpet bedding craze that dismantled the English gardens that had encapsulated the sum total of Western horticulture to that point. In the only land where Pliny's idea to see the countryside as part of the garden itself had actually taken hold, the vistas were now replete with geometric blocks of primary colours.

If tropical annuals of the Americas wreaked the revenge of the Incas and Aztecs—by allowing the Victorians to take their bedding schemes to their logical extreme—it was the English, not the Spanish, who had paid the price. I feel indebted, however, to the Incas for the seed heads they bred from wild sunflowers, and even more grateful for cultivating *Theobroma cacao*, the source of chocolate, which they sensibly called "food of the gods."

The English flower garden, as we know it, was born essentially during the Renaissance. During the perilous Middle Ages, beauty had taken a back seat to survival. Stability and prosperity allowed the time to create a "Garden of Pleasant Flowers," as John Parkinson described in 1627, in his *Paradisi in Sole, Paradisus Terrestris*, the first book solely about ornamental plants. Until that point, English gardeners valued plants most highly for their medicinal properties, although even the great herbalists like William Turner and John Gerard pointed out the beauty and sweet smells of favourite flowers in landmark volumes first printed in 1551 and 1583, respectively.

A manuscript from the fifteenth century, now in the British Museum, contains a list of plants deemed necessary for the garden. While the list relied heavily on the simples for medicine and cooking, a few plants with only modest practical use, but fair in flower, were included. Even six hundred years ago, it was unthinkable to exclude violets, daisies, poppies, primroses, and lilies from the garden. The foundation for the gardens of Parkinson's day had been laid by Chaucer's words in "The Frankeleyn's Tale":

This gardeyn full of leves and of flowres:
And craft of mannes hand so curiously
Arrayed hadde this garden, trewely,
That nevere was ther garden of swich prys,
But if it were the verray paradys.

The English have long been gardeners first, and garden designers second. With the exception of a giant national hiccup known as the Victorian age, English gardeners have always been more interested in the plants themselves than in the design of the garden where they are grown. This trait is particularly apparent when comparing the English and the French. Versailles is widely held to be the greatest achievement in formal gardening. Its architect, André Le Nôtre, lamented that upstairs maids would probably be the only ones to closely observe its intricate parterres. The flowers embedded in the parterres, designed for nobles to view from upstairs windows of the palace, were far less important than Louis's presumed triumph over nature.

By contrast, English monarchs never built anything as radical as Versailles. They modified and embellished the gardens of their predecessors. Many of the kings and queens took an active role in gardening and cherished particular flowers. Queen Elizabeth I loved flowers and wore them in her hair and on her robes.

Norsemen and Danes brought the flowers of their homelands to English shores, where they became wild. The Normans introduced what was to become the quintessential country flower, the pink. Plant hunting throughout the world became a national quest in the centuries to come. Bleeding Heart and Balloon Flower came to symbolize the flora of the cottage garden far better than their Oriental countries of origin.

Brilliant *Lobelia cardinalis*, RIGHT, thrives in moist ground.

THE AMERICAN EXPERIMENT

It is to England and other European nations we look for the foundations of the Western gardening tradition. American horticulture, in turn, traces its roots to the Old World. Early gardens in America were simple affairs. Those of the loyal, home-loving English were formal, if without embellishment. The Puritan settlers, who might be characterized as ideological refugees, had little desire to reproduce the pretty tricks of ostentatious design representative of all they had left behind. No knot gardens or clipped parterres, no boxwood maze or clipped topiary would be planted in their New World.

Instead, the Puritan garden was orderly but simple, and probably resembled the English cottage garden of today, the roots of which also can be traced at least to the Elizabethan age. The housewife tended a variety of flowers and herbs, and everything she needed she grew herself: plants for seasoning food, for treating illness and wounds, for repelling insects, and for deodorants. The simples—flowering herbs—were the staples of her garden. But she had also brought flowers without healing properties to comfort her, such as favourite pinks, violets, and pansies.

The pretty orange flowers of Pot Marigold, *Calendula officinalis*, might have reminded her of home. Distilled marigold water could be applied to a lady's forehead to relieve a headache, as she might have read in *The Queens Closet* by Nathaniel Brooks. This 1658 volume, when opened, revealed "Incomporable Secrets in Physick, Chyrurgery, Preserving, Candying and Cooking" and could scarcely be kept in stock by Boston booksellers. A recipe for "water of life" to treat ills ranging from palsy to worms, could be concocted from the garden. It included—among thirty-three ingredients—thyme, rosemary, tarragon, hyssop, carnations, roses, and fennel, as well as mutton, eggs, sugar, and bread. We might conclude that the resulting mud was thicker than water. A mangy dog, the book advised, could be treated with a similar everything-but-the-kitchen-sink ointment. The main ingredients were tar and grease, but brimstone, gunpowder, and honey were also vital components of the mixture, and the so-treated dog was to be tied in the sun to hasten a cure. Dogs were somewhat scarce in seventeenth-century New England.

Pretty wildflowers of the new continent quickly found a place in the garden of the New England housewife, and soon in English soil. Thirty species of North American plants grew there by 1600. Among them were corn, *Zea mays*, Canadian Columbine, *Aquilegia canadensis*, Jerusalem Artichoke, *Helianthus tuberosus* (though its origin could not be discerned by its name), and Pearl Everlasting, *Anaphalis margaritacea* (to which Gerard gave the less-than-poetic name Cudweede of America). In a letter to John Winthrop, "governor of new Inglande," in 1637, Sir Drew Deane asks that "if you find any curious flowers to favour me with some." A tradition of welcoming new flowers continued, and a national appetite for American ones had been whetted.

NEW ENGLAND NATURALISTS

At the same time, some European flowers had already achieved wild status in the colonies. John Josselyn, an English traveller and chronicler, listed in 1672 twenty-three "such Plants as have sprung up since the English Planted and kept cattle in New England." So abundant are the flowers today in the wild, that only the denotation "naturalized" or "introduced" distinguishes them in botanical guidebooks. Ox-eye daisies and buttercups, seemingly among the most native of American wildflowers, most likely secured passage to America in colonial cattle feed.

Josselyn visited New England twice. His second trip, in 1633, lasted eight years. He published *New-Englands Rarities Discovered* in 1672 and *An Account of Two Voyages to New England* three years later. These volumes not only provide an insight into the traditional plants grown in the colonies, but they detail the "rarities" he found. He was the first naturalist to describe Skunk Cabbage and Pitcher Plant. Of the latter, the genus *Sarracenia*, he was amazed to find something so "fantastick" of a flower to have gone unnoticed.

Josselyn's words were eagerly read, as had been those in William Wood's *New England Prospect* in 1634. European naturalists and botanists flocked to the new land. The French sent home seeds and specimens from Canada, which is why so many New England wildflowers bear the botanical epithet "of Canada," such as *Aquilegia canadensis*, *Asarum canadense*, *Cornus canadensis* and *Lilium canadense*. Probably the first garden planted in the Northeast in the seventeenth century was by Champlain and his

The species *Aquilegia canadensis*, ABOVE, was discovered by 1640. *Echinocystis lobata*, BELOW, is called Mock Cucumber. Early gardens were simple, RIGHT.

company in New France, now part of the state of Maine. The Dutch and Spanish had holdings in North America as well, but the largest repository for flowers from the New World was the Chelsea Physic Garden in London.

The first native American botanist was John Bartram. His farm near Philadelphia, begun in 1728, might be considered the first botanic garden in the New World. The most influential naturalists in the land, Bartram and his son, William, botanized from Florida to Canada. On one such trip in 1756, they discovered an unknown tree on the Altamaha River near Fort Barrington, Georgia. They collected seed, naming it *Franklinia* for their friend and fellow naturalist, Benjamin Franklin. The beautiful white-flowering tree thrived in cultivation, as it does still, but disappeared from the wild. It was last seen in the same area as reported by the Bartrams in 1803, and is believed to be extinct in the wild.

The first woman botanist in America was Jane Colden, who in the mid–eighteenth century wrote and illustrated a flora, a botanic study, of New York. European botanists were somewhat surprised to discover a talented colleague in the trans-Atlantic wilderness, let alone a woman. Englishman Peter Collinson, an enthusiast of American wildflowers and friend of Bartram, wrote in a letter from 1758 to Linnaeus, "As this accomplished lady is the only one of the fair sex that I have heard of, who is scientifically skillful in the Linnaean system, you will no doubt distinguish her merits, and recommend her example to the ladies of every country."

THE FINAL FRONTIER

The American Revolution altered the course of botany from dominantly English contacts to internal, as well as French ones. André Michaux was sent by his government in 1785 to gather seeds of plants of economic importance for timber, medicine, and crops. He loved flowers, however, and managed to discover several wildflowers that bear his name. It was partly his *Flora boreali-Americana*, with plates by Jean-Pierre Redouté, that spurred American interest in discovering wildflowers.

Professor Benjamin Smith Barton of Philadelphia commenced work on a North American flora. His apprentice and collector, Thomas Nuttall, visited an enormous area to collect specimens for him. Nuttall eventually became curator of the Harvard Botanical Gardens, but, being shy, was ill at ease in the university community. He cut a trap door in his bedroom closet to descend into his study below, so as not to meet people in the hallway, and he took his meals through a sliding panel. What he lacked in the social graces, Nuttall compensated for by being the foremost collector of his era. Asa Gray would later proclaim, ". . . few naturalists have ever excelled him in aptitude for such observations, in quickness of eye, tact, in

discrimination and tenacity of memory."

When the authorities at Harvard refused Nuttall's request for a leave of absence to join an expedition to the West, he resigned. During his resulting travels he discovered many new wildflowers, including species of *Viola*, *Gilia*, *Helianthus*, and *Oenothera*. He named a perennial species of *Zinnia* found growing in Colorado *grandiflora*, although the pretty yellow blossoms measure less than an inch across.

Even before Congress had approved the funds, Thomas Jefferson had written secretly to Professor Barton, asking him to prepare notes on botany and zoology for an exploring party to the West. The purchase of the Louisiana Territory had made it vital for Jefferson to know more about the lands that lay across the Mississippi River. He appointed his secretary, Meriwether Lewis, to lead the expedition, with Lewis's army buddy, William Clark, as co-leader. The pair led the first American crossing, starting in 1804, of the continent north of Mexico, and gave credence to the United States claim to the Oregon territory. They blazed a trail from St. Louis, Missouri, to the Pacific Ocean.

The story of the Lewis and Clark crossing is an incredible one, as the 32 men, one woman, and one baby crossed 4000 uncharted miles through the Dakotas, Montana, Idaho, Washington, and Oregon. The entire 7700-mile round trip from St. Louis to the coast and back, which began in 1804, took two years, four months, and

Thomas Nuttall named *Zinnia grandiflora*, LEFT. **Country flowers, including *Lobelia siphilitica* and *Sedum spectabile*,** are welcome indoors, RIGHT.

eleven days. Remarkably, only one man died, and his death was caused by a ruptured appendix. The fabled Native American woman, Sacajawea (meaning bird woman), served as an interpreter. Perhaps even more importantly, her presence—with her very young child—gave the party a vivid outward appearance of a peaceful band, and did much to ease their passage. Though no wildflower bears her name, Bird Woman Falls in Glacier National Park acknowledges her contribution. A glossy technicolor motion picture version of the story, called *The Far Horizons*, (1955) should be taken with a grain of salt. The casting of Donna Reed as Sacajawea should alert, if not alarm, the viewer.

The leaders of the expedition are immortalized by two charming wildflowers that they found. The star-shaped blossoms of *Lewisia*, called Bitterroot, hug the ground in western high country; the elegant sprays of *Clarkia*, often called Rocky Mountain Garland, tint the forest's edge in the Northwest. Altogether, Lewis and Clark added more than two hundred new species to the inventory of wildflowers, including four new genera.

An epoch of Western exploration had begun, as party after party set off for the wilderness. Expeditions led by Zebulon Pike, Stephen Long, John Fremont, John Gunnison, and many more crossed the plains and traversed the Rocky Mountains. More often than not, the leader would get a mountain named for him. Two impressive Colorado peaks bear the names Torrey and Gray. The adjoining fourteen-thousand-footers are named for Dr. John Torrey and Dr. Asa Gray, not explorers, but botanists. Most of the new finds of flora from Western excursions were sent back to them. Torrey taught at Columbia University (and later, at Princeton), and hired Gray to assist him as a collector, and later, as collaborator. Their association was a long and fruitful one, and they were considered the last word on American plants from the 1820's until Torrey's death in 1873, and Gray's in 1888. Gray later became a professor at Harvard, where he put immeasurable effort into meshing American botany with the European effort. The two shared a unique window in botanic history, as the treasures of the West came to light. They inspected and consequently named species discovered during virtually every government expedition into the American West for fifty years.

Both men visited Colorado separately in

Wild westerners include California Poppy, BELOW, and *Brodiaea laxa*, RIGHT.

WESTWARD THE WAGONS

During Jefferson's lifetime, 1743 to 1826, the population of the country increased tenfold. As settlers headed west across the American continent, they did so with carefully wrapped pots and scions of fruiting vines, trees, and shrubs, as well as cherished perennials and annuals. The journeys were arduous and perilous. Over burdened wagons made slow progress through the wilderness. The Oregon Trail was littered with cast-off furniture, sets of china, and all-but-essential goods. It must have been heartbreaking to abandon family heirlooms and favourite peonies and lilacs to lighten the load. The California Trail was strewn with similar castoffs and the occasional ominous bleached skull of a steer, as depicted in Westerns. Weather, rattlesnakes, and war parties took their toll. Not every journey was completed.

Even so, prairie homesteads and new settlements soon bloomed with the flowers that had survived the trips (with their owners), and the pretty new wildflowers that settlers discovered growing about their new homes. Old photographs show determined pioneer women posing with hollyhocks as backdrops. Civilization, and its accompanying gardens, had arrived in the Wild West, for better or worse.

It is sobering to contemplate how four hundred years of civilization have brought more changes to the American continent than any other four centuries in the world's history. From a primeval forest of exceptional variety, the land has been reduced by European tools to wood lots and second growth. Species of birds and mammals were hunted to extinction, while some native flowers perished before they could be named. The American experiment continues.

Firewheel and Calliopsis grow together, BELOW.

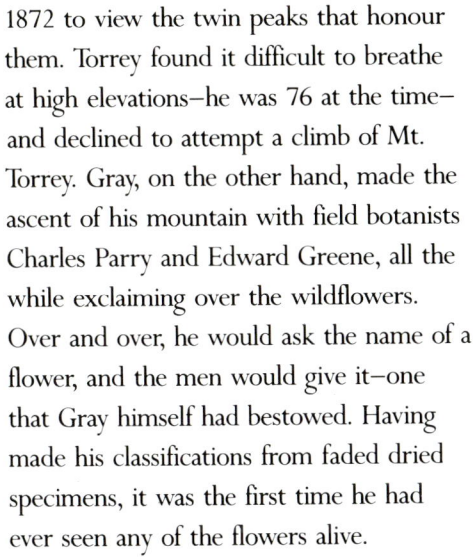

1872 to view the twin peaks that honour them. Torrey found it difficult to breathe at high elevations—he was 76 at the time—and declined to attempt a climb of Mt. Torrey. Gray, on the other hand, made the ascent of his mountain with field botanists Charles Parry and Edward Greene, all the while exclaiming over the wildflowers. Over and over, he would ask the name of a flower, and the men would give it—one that Gray himself had bestowed. Having made his classifications from faded dried specimens, it was the first time he had ever seen any of the flowers alive.

CHAPTER TWO

GREEN CARGOES

Strangely enough, when a flower escapes from the garden into the freedom of wood or field, it is looked on with suspicion and distrust. This point of view is difficult to understand, and the term "probably an escape," or still worse, "a garden stray" (like a poor, unwanted cat), coming at the end of a description of some flower in a botanical book, should surely read something like this: "This beautiful flower, escaping with difficulty over the garden wall, has, by its intrepid spirit and power of overcoming uncongenial climatic conditions and unaccustomed pests, greatly added to the beauty and interest of the countryside."

Ethel Armitage **A Country Garden**

THROUGHOUT THE HISTORY OF horticulture—which parallels the history of civilization itself—mankind has tamed wild plants. Ancient humans selected grains to eat and fibre plants for weaving into clothing. Mankind discovered wheat at a fortuitous time for both species. The original wild wheat, probably a chance hybrid between two grasses, prospered under cultivation, producing more seeds through careful selection and benefitting from having competing plants eradicated. Wheat needed human cultivation to survive, for

the heavy grains in the seed heads drop and germinate closely together, where it is too crowded for any of the seedlings to survive. The seeds must be sown annually, carefully spaced, to insure a harvest, as well as the survival of the species, for wild wheat has long been extinct.

When the human hand touches a plant, it sets in motion a chain of irrevocable events. It may signal an opportunity for the plant to expand its range, or it may mean a transformation as natural selection is hurried or perverted. It may even spell extinction, as a plant is obliterated to make room for another.

As humans have migrated about the globe, they have carried with them, purposely or not, plants native to their former homes. Some species adapt and thrive; others wither and die. These "green cargoes" change the face of the lands on which they land. In their homelands, most flowers are kept in check by the complex ecosystems in which they have evolved. A natural system of control governs the fortunes of plant and animal life. Natural predators and diseases restrain each species. Released from the confines of their native habitats, however, some plants and animals sweep through virgin territories like Mongol hordes.

Most of the invaders into England were gentle ones. Jupiter's-beard, *Centranthus ruber*, probably crossed the English Channel during Roman occupations; few gardeners complain of its introduction. The arrival of the Martagon Lily was so unheralded that many have thought it to be a native, albeit rare, wildflower. Gerard described the central European lily, erroneously, as indigenous to Syria and "such hot countries as do border upon Morea and Greece, many daies journies beyond Constantinople. . . ."

Romans probably introduced Centranthus ruber to England where it established a tenacious hold, ABOVE.

THE INVASION OF AMERICA

Green cargoes entered the American continent from several ports of entry. English settlers took their gardens with them, and the most adaptable flowers established themselves throughout the countryside from Maine to Virginia. Yarrow and Elecampane, Feverfew, St.-John's-wort, and Chicory bloom in pastures and along roads, standing shoulder-to-shoulder with true native flowers. Bouncing Bet, Chamomile, and Lily of the Valley announce sites of abandoned gardens, while *Rosa rugosa* blooms above their heads. The wine-pink blossoms of Ragged Robin, *Lychnis flos-cuculi*, and yellow Fleur-de-lis, *Iris pseudacorus*, dot moist meadows. The little yellow broom, *Genista tinctoria*, was used by colonial women to dye cloth; its escape to Gallows Hill in Salem earned it the folk name Witches Blood.

On the other side of the vast new land, the Spanish had already forever-altered the face of the West. Setting out from Mexico City in 1540, Francisco Vasques de Coronado intended to conquer the gold-laden Seven Cities of Cibola and, perhaps, to find their fabled shaggy cows, *las vacas de Cibola*. The cities of legend were found by Coronado to be pueblos of the Zuni; the inhabitants wore turquoise and abalone beads, not gold, and they kept no herds of buffalo. His 300 horsemen, 800 footmen, and the herds of cattle and sheep they drove to feed the army, left a trail of introduced species of flowers. Dandelions, common Mallow, Lamb's Quarters, and my accursed Puncture Vine are their living legacy.

OVERSTAYING THEIR WELCOME

Some introductions to America have been disastrous, though no land has been immune. Wives of English governors, transporting their flowers from outpost to outpost in far flung dominions of the Empire, have unwittingly been responsible for some of the horticultural invasions. A single blueberry bush in New Zealand today covers more than a mile of beach. The British Isles received a scourge or two as

well. *Aegopodium podagraria*, the so-called Bishop's Weed (though a more unholy plant can scarcely be imagined) came to England with the Romans under the guise of being a cure for gout (a disease by which the over-indulgent religious hierarchy might have been plagued). Unfortunately, the cure for a garden infested

The pale blossoms of Chicory, *Cichorium intybus*, LEFT and ABOVE, open in the morning in a 'countrified' city garden.

GREEN CARGOES

with it has not yet been discovered.

More than two millennia later, Kudzu Vine, *Pueraria lobata*, was imported from Japan to the southern United States to help control soil erosion. This it did, and more, smothering all in its expanding path with dark green leaves. Kudzu, by the way, can supposedly be planted without fear in areas of freezing winter temperatures. Those who have witnessed the vine engulfing entire Georgian farms—house, barn, and silo—and who have slow-moving pets or grandparents, are understandably wary of introducing the energetic vines. Kudzu is being planted experimentally in New York; if a hardy form is found, the Empire State Building may face a more determined climber than King Kong.

Tumbleweeds, *Amaranthus albus*, roll picturesquely past saloons in scenes from old Westerns. They are less romantic images to farmers and ranchers, who have fought the rolling advance since the seed of the Siberian immigrants first stowed away in sacks of grain. I recall a fierce windstorm one night as a child, when the hedges on either side of our house served as a giant funnel for the tumbleweeds. When I woke in the morning, the room was strangely dark, and tumbleweeds blocked my windows. Upstairs, the windows were similarly obscured. Rushing through the front door (the back one would not open), we discovered a tangle of tumbleweeds rising as high as the chimney. Thousands of them were piled behind the house for fifty feet. My father cleared and burnt them for days (at a safe distance from the house, lest he ignite a bonfire of epic proportions).

Some introduced plants are merely nuisances by comparison. Dandelions forged a two-pronged assault on America, having been introduced by Coronado in the West and Puritans in the East. Barely a lawn of Kentucky bluegrass in America doesn't sprout them each spring. Curiously, children love dandelions; only later, when they grow up to have their own lawns, do they worry about keeping up appearances and getting rid of them. The English feel the same about their pretty little lawn weed, *Bellis perennis*. "The lawn is very gay with daisies," wrote Ethel Armitage one May, "which is just what it should not be." An old children's rhyme tells the story:

> *I am a pretty thing,*
> *I wear a ruby ring,*
> *My heart is gold.*
>
> *And though men tread on me,*
> *The Children stoop to see*
> *My buds unfold.*
>
> *Watching till I am grown*
> *To be a flower full blown,*
> *Then take me.*
>
> *With nimble fingers they*
> *Into a necklace gay*
> *Do make me.*

The jury is still out on Purple Loosestrife, *Lythrum salicaria*. Introduced from Europe, the moisture-loving perennial, bearing tall spikes of tiny purple flowers, invaded the wetlands of New England and the upper Midwest. The plant is banned for importation into many states, and so are supposedly infertile hybrids. The haze of purple flowers makes a beguiling picture, reflected on the mirrored surfaces of ponds and marshes, but at the expense of native plants whose place *L. salicaria* has usurped. In my urban garden, where the closest wetland is several hundred miles away, and the average rainfall is a scant fourteen inches annually, Purple Loosestrife is a model of decorum. It would not survive without supplemental irrigation, and the challenge has been to keep it alive, not to keep it in check.

The Tawny Daylily, *Hemerocallis fulva*, is thought by many country visitors to be a native flower in America. It was introduced from China where it is cultivated for its tasty tubers rather than its orange flowers. Wild again in a new land—a survivor from gardens planted around vanished farmhouses or cabins—it is estimated that there are more Tawny Daylilies growing wild in the United States than in all of China. This does not even take into account the legions of daylily hybrids found in gardens coast-to-coast.

Farmers, too, have a different perspective than gardeners. A postcard-pretty field of golden grain, overrun with scarlet poppies, delights all but the dismayed English farmer. Long despised by farmers as well, *Centaurea cyanus* was branded with the name Hurt Sickle because it blunted the farmer's blades. Gardeners prefer the more charming names of Cornflower, Ragged Sailor, Bluebottle, or Bachelor's Button, depending where they grew up. Corn Cockle, *Agrostemma githago*, is a delight in the flower bed and a terror in the field. Its seeds, when unwittingly harvested and milled with the grain, ruin the flour with their taste and those who eat the bread develop, at the very least, indigestion.

Lovely as it is, European *Lythrum salicaria*, ABOVE, spreads unchecked in wetlands.

THE NEW WAVE

Invasions continue to this day despite stringent efforts at control. The horticultural ones are at least not as frightening as the animal ones. I have nightmares imagining fire ants, walking lungfish, killer bees, and Mediterranean fruit flies converging on my garden. Southern states seem to get the worst of these pests, both plant and beast, but sometimes the results are not all that disastrous. Miami is adopted home to the Canary Island Date Palm and the Canary-winged Parakeet. Brought together from opposite sides of the Atlantic, the South American escapees from the exotic pet trade found appropriate nesting in the palms, and abundant food in the other exotic species grown in southern Florida. Though they flock in screeching groups and have gluttonous appetites, the public is thus far enthusiastic about the pretty little parrots that sleep upside down in the stately palms.

Gardeners often import green cargoes with unusual results. The Aspen Valley of Colorado only recently became home to a new immigrant. As the recent vogue for wild gardening expanded, seed companies offered "wild flower mixes" throughout the country. Some seed mixtures are more appropriate for some areas than others, and those appropriate for mountain areas, containing true native wildflowers, are rare. Bachelor's Button and Corn Poppy, however charming, are not indigenous to the western slope of Colorado. But these annual flowers do no harm and rarely persist for more than a few pretty years.

What has remained from these meadow mixtures, however, is Tansy, *Tanacetum vulgare*. This yellow-flowered European native came to America with colonists as one of the simples. It escaped into the wild country of New England, where it seems a fitting relic of colonial days. In Colorado, the towering herb appears incongruous among the alpine flora. Perhaps, in several hundred years, Tansy will be accepted as an old-time resident, a souvenir of the ski boom.

Tansy was introduced to America by settlers, ABOVE, and escaped into the wild, LEFT.

CHAPTER THREE

A GARDEN FROM THE WILDERNESS

A PROPHET IS NOT WITHOUT HONOR SAVE IN HIS OWN COUNTRY; TRUE IS THIS SAYING WHEN RENDERED—A PLANT IS NOT WANTING ADMIRATION SAVE IN ITS NATIVE LAND.

F. Lamson Scribner
Ornamental and Useful Plants of Maine (1874)

AMERICA BLOOMS WITH lovely wildflowers. It is a land of incredible diversity, and yet for hundreds of years American gardeners imported ornamental plants from Europe while largely ignoring their own. Conversely, American wildflowers have been all the rage in England since father and son John Tradescant first introduced goldenrods and spiderworts (appropriately named *Tradescantia* in their honour) from Virginia about 1640.

Andrew Jackson Downing chastised his American countrymen about 1850 in the *Horticulturist*, "Nothing strikes foreign horticulturists and amateurs so much as this apathy and indifference of Americans to the beautiful sylvan and floral products of their own country. An enthusiastic collector in Belgium first made us keenly sensible of this condition of our countryman, last summer, in describing the difficulty he had in procuring from any of his correspondents here, American seeds or plants, even of well known and tolerably abundant species, by telling us that amateurs and nurserymen who annually import from him every new and rare exotic that the

Joe Pye Weed grows at pondside, BELOW.

Artemisia and Rudbeckia grace a wild garden, LEFT.

richest collections of Europe possessed, could scarcely be prevailed upon to make a search for native American plants, far more beautiful, which grow in the woods not ten miles from their own doors. Some of them were wholly ignorant of such plants, except so far as a familiarity with their names in the books may be called an acquaintance. Others knew them, but considered them 'wild plants,' and therefore, too little deserving of attention to be worth the trouble of collecting, even for curious foreigners. And so" he continued, "in a country of azaleas, kalmias, rhododendrons, cypripediums, magnolias and nyssas—the loveliest flowers, shrubs, and trees of the temperate climates—you never put them in your gardens, but send over the water every year for thousands of dollars worth of English larches and Dutch hyacinths. Voilà le goût Républicain!"

Downing certainly hit the nail on the head, albeit in some very long sentences. Even though his words were written nearly 150 years ago, I blushed scarlet when I read them; I always do when I'm scolded. Gardeners hate being scolded,

A GARDEN FROM THE WILDERNESS 43

however, and when lectured about what they should be growing, most of them will grow just the opposite. Gardening, like any other form of art, is subject to the whims of fashion. There is no right way to garden, or wrong way, for that matter. There are no correct plants to grow, all advice to the contrary. Gardeners make their own decisions about what pleases them most. There is no moral imperative to grow the wildflowers of one's region, but some have found pleasure in doing so through the years. Gardeners have traditionally learned by observation and have been swayed by those considered to have "taste," or at least the wherewithal to hire someone with it. Flowers that have fallen out of fashion, or have never achieved fashionable status in the first place, need the stamp of approval from a tastemaker. In American horticulture, the role has traditionally been played by someone foreign, often British.

Transformed only by words of praise from English writers, some American plants occasionally were readmitted to gardens in this country with new respectability, like a girl returning from finishing school. Gertrude Jekyll grew yuccas "in bold patches the whole fifteen-feet of the border," though in America they are rarely seen save for clichéd groupings with wagon wheels at dude ranches. "They look good at all times of the year because of their grand strong foliage," proclaimed the artistic Englishwoman, "and they are the glory of the garden when in flower."

"There is a quiet beauty about the more select Starworts," said William Robinson about New England's asters, "which is charming in the autumn days, and their variety of colour, of form, and of bud and blossoms is delightful."

Other plants have not been showered with such superlatives, especially natives that demanded exacting requirements to thrive. Most of the penstemons, for example, a grand New World genus that have evolved under blazing summer sun, tend to sulk in maritime mildness. Some flowers refuse to be tamed in any garden. Indian Paintbrushes (*Castilleja*) splash hillsides and mountains of the Rockies with broad sweeps of orange, red, pink, and white flowers; but because they require companion grasses or artemisias (on whose roots the Indian Paintbrushes are partly parasitic) to thrive, they are difficult to cultivate. The host plant must grow where the seeds of the paintbrush are germinated or the paintbrush and companion must be transplanted together.

Many wildflowers cannot, and should not, be transplanted from the wild for similar reasons. Those that rely on a specific habitat often have a complex nutritional association with a specific fungus that lives in the roots of the plant. Lady-slipper Orchids are an excellent example. Understanding the requirements of this fungus is beyond the scope of most gardeners, and when it dies, so does the Lady-slipper. The rarest of wildflowers are protected by law, so digging or picking them is not only immoral, it's illegal.

*Species of *Eriogonum*, LEFT, ABOVE, and *Castilleja*, LEFT, BELOW, grow in the American West. *Rudbeckia triloba*, *Eupatorium purpureum*, and *Vernonia noveboracensis* thrive in the East, RIGHT.*

44 Wild Flowers

REGIONAL BLOSSOMS

Happily, many country flowers, native and introduced, can be grown under widely divergent conditions. Understanding the regional wildflower communities enables a gardener to provide the type of conditions likely to ensure success with a particular flower.

Over one hundred specialized plant communities are recognized in the continental United States, while there are fewer but equally diverse communities in the United Kingdom. The native flora of these communities have adapted through time to each particular combination of climate and soil. Substantial differences might seem to preclude any sort of common ground, so to speak. Some plants are of such an adaptable nature, however, that they transcend many climatic differences with little effort. Scarcely an American or British gardener cannot grow Sea Pink, Black-eyed

Susan, New England Aster, or most of the flowers found throughout these pages. We truly share common ground.

Gardeners, to some degree, are able to control light, soil, and moisture to simulate that of the native environs of flowers they wish to grow. In my urban garden, for example, specific areas imitate particular habitats—woodland, meadow, alpine, wetland, and plain.

Success may be had by catering to the needs of the wildflowers from a significantly different climate. Colonial gardeners learned early on to build raised beds to provide adequate drainage for the Mediterranean herbs that rotted from wintertime wet feet. Gardeners in semi-arid lands have learned to find microclimates in the garden where woodland flowers will thrive. Low-lying areas and artificial water features can accommodate natives from streambank and brookside. Soil amendments, such as peat moss to acidify the soil, can be made to meet the needs of particular plants.

GARDENING IN STYLE

It is unlikely that the style of the gardens in which most country flowers are grown will influence their performance in any way. Writers often speak of "how natural" a flower may appear in a particular spot, or "how suited" a plant seems for a particular use. Some flowers thrive best in gardens of a certain style because the horticultural practices accompanying that style best suit their needs. There is no secret, nor shame, in admitting that cosmos will thrive for a negligent gardener better than roses. An overzealous gardener, on the other hand, may well drown the Blazing Star, *Mentzelia laevicaulis*, or Wine Cup, *Callirhoe involucrata*, with too much kindness.

The joy of country flowers is their adaptability, although there are limits, of course. While retaining the wild charm for which we value them, these flowers grace designs from formal to naturalistic. Gayfeather is as pretty in parterres as it is in a grand border or small bed. Indian Blanket is as appropriate surrounding a Massachusetts colonial home as it is in a prairie garden of a ranch house in Wyoming. Turtle-head grows in country gardens and in urban ones in the most crowded cities.

Gardening style is a personal matter, but the most prevalent modes bear labels. Perennial borders, no matter their shape or size, are a popular aspiration. The tradi-

Jewel Weed, *Impatiens capensis*, threads through grasses, LEFT. **Perennials interlock in a border,** RIGHT.

tional form, irregularly planted, takes a hedge or fence as a backdrop, but sometimes it spills out into a lawn, amoeba-shape, when it is rechristened as an island bed (although some of these are merely peninsulas). Sometimes this flattens out entirely, incorporating the grasses, and becomes a meadow. The only real distinction seems to be the number of weeds that are overlooked. Taller versions are called prairie or wilderness gardens. If it is full of bugs and rodents, it is a naturalist's garden. When this becomes overstuffed with as many plants as possible, and the house begins to disappear behind a curtain of green, the gardener has created a cottage garden, even if the dwelling itself is the size of the White House.

Cottage gardens are treated with near reverence by some, and the informal and unpretentious plantings have made an enormous impression on garden style. They were an inspiration to Gertrude Jekyll, Margery Fish, and many others down to this day. They are, according to Christopher Lloyd, "an excuse for legitimized messiness with flopping masses of uncontrolled vegetation." Perhaps, though, the cottage style has encouraged many a gardener to become more horticulturally active, without fear of becoming slave to a garden that needs all available spare time to appear respectable. Not that cottage gardens are labour-saving, but they can be ignored for periods of time when necessary without going completely to ruin. Dedicated collectors, whose gardens in the past were considered almost outside the realm of fine gardening, can be judged

A wild look is achieved, LEFT. An island bed, ABOVE, takes centre stage. BELOW, grey foliage accents flowers.

now by their achievements, not by their adherence to a school of design.

Confessions by "magpie gardeners," in whose gardens country flowers often abound, speak to the collector in all of us. Allen Lacy claims to "have an abstract knowledge of the virtues of restraint," and has read, by his own admission, the works of Vita Sackville-West and Christopher Lloyd, and made pilgrimages to their gardens as well. "But having the benefit of good advice," writes Lacy, "is no assurance that it will be followed. Ever since St. Augustine's *Confessions*, we've known that it's one thing to *know* what's good and another to *do* it, so it should be no surprise that *my* garden is a mess, if considered according to its overall design."

If there has ever been a garden writer who enjoyed a garden more than Lacy does his, I would be hard-pressed to name him or her. I do, however, know dozens of ordinary dirt gardeners who enjoy their creations as much. Some of them strive for something of great artistry, often-as-not achieving it, but they do not approach design with the deliberation of making nuclear weapons. They indulge their whims, laugh at their failures, and get on with it.

I've never met a gardener who didn't think a favourite, particularly demanding flower well worth all the effort. Better to have loved and lost—and so on—applies to many of us and our horticultural quests. Growing flowers, as man has done since the first blossoms were dug from the wild, combines skill, artistry, and improvisation. Happenstance is sometimes the very best of designers.

A cottage garden, LEFT, teems with plants. Conductors slow their trains to view poppies and flax, ABOVE.

CHAPTER FOUR

A PORTFOLIO OF ANTIQUE SPECIES

> They admonish and stir up a man to that which is comelie and honest; for flowers through their beautie, varietie of colour and exquisite forme doe bring to a liberall and gentlemanly mind, the remembrance of honestie, comeliness and all kinds of virtues.
>
> John Gerard

Anemone Ranunculaceae

Anemone canadensis
CANADIAN ANEMONE

Anemone × hybrida
JAPANESE WINDFLOWER

Anemone sylvestris
SNOWDROP WINDFLOWER

Anemone virginiana
THIMBLEWEED

Anemones are called windflowers or Daughters of the Wind, explained by herbalist William Turner in 1551, because "the floure never openeth it self, but when the wynde bloweth." Nicholas Culpeper used the same explanation in 1653 noting that, "Pliny is my author; if it be not so, blame him." So much for honour among herbalists. The name *Anemone* is probably of Semitic origin, from *Na'man*, meaning Adonis (we must trust the linguists here). The spillage of his blood created two new flowers, the *Anemone* as well as the *Adonis*. The blood red flowers of *A. coronaria* were woven by the Greeks and Romans into garlands. This *Anemone* species was grown in England at a very early date, possibly arriving with the Romans, and later became a favourite florist's flower.

When John Gerard wrote his herbal in 1597, he boasted that "Myselfe have in my garden twelve different sorts; and yet I do heare of . . . more, differing very notably from any of these; every new yeare bringeth with it new and strange kinds; and every country peculiar plants of this sort. . . ." Indeed, more than a hundred species of *Anemone*, a genus of the Buttercup family, inhabit northern temperate and arctic regions of the entire globe.

Snowdrop Windflower, *A. sylvestris*, grows wild from eastern Europe into Sweden and France. This spring bloomer is cherished for its sweetly scented, luminous white flowers held above the foliage on long, wiry stems. European settlers in America discovered counterparts in their new land, such as *A. canadensis*. It has similar white flowers, and is widely distributed in moist woodlands from Quebec to British Columbia, extending south to Missouri and New Mexico. Native Americans used the leaves and roots to treat nosebleeds and sores, and made an eyewash, for twitching and crossed eyes, from them.

A. virginiana delighted colonists on the eastern seaboard with its stiff-stemmed, green-tinted flowers. The distinctively shaped seed cone earned it the colloquial name Thimbleweed. Native Americans used it to treat whooping cough and tuberculosis. The unconscious could be revived by blowing the smoke of burning seeds into their nostrils. Thimbleweed grows in dry and open woodlands from Canada to Alabama, and as far west as Arkansas. This adaptability recommends it for planting in many regional gardens. Like most of the other species, it thrives in partial shade in humus-enriched soil, though, like the others, it will succeed planted in full sun if abundant moisture is available.

Thimbleweed combines with Elecampane and Old Gooseneck, FAR LEFT, and in a wildflower bouquet, LEFT. Japanese Anemone, ABOVE, blooms late. ILLUSTRATION, *A. sylvestris*.

Gardens of the western world would surely be the poorer in autumn without the Japanese Anemone. Despite its name, this *Anemone* is native to China and was introduced to Japan at a very early point; the date is lost in time. A German living in Nagasaki first described the plant about 1685, and confusion has reigned since. Since no European was allowed to venture further than the vicinity of two or three ports inland into China or Japan at that time, and for several centuries more, botanists were unable to ascertain the truth.

English plant hunter Robert Fortune sent the first living plant to the Horticultural Society in 1844 from China. He found it "in full flower among the graves of the natives, which are round the ramparts of Shanghae; it blooms in November when other flowers have gone by, and is a most appropriate ornament to the last resting-places of the dead."

Fortune's cultivated form of the wild *A. hupehensis* (named for the Chinese province of Hupeh) was crossed early on with the species *A. vitifolia*, which had been secured in Nepal in 1829 by Lady Amherst. The resulting hybrid, properly called *A.* × *hybrida*, fostered an entire race of so-called Japanese anemones. In 1851, a French nurseryman discovered a root branch of a plant that bloomed with pure white flowers. Detached and propagated, the sport was named for his daughter. 'Honorine Jobert' is still considered by many to be the loveliest of the Japanese anemones.

Aquilegia Ranunculaceae

A. caerulea is arranged with Feverfew and Burnett, ABOVE.
A. caerulea grows with *Campanula latiloba*, RIGHT. ILLUSTRATION, *A. vulgaris*.

It is a commonly held belief that the name *Aquilegia* is derived from the Latin *aquila*, an eagle, from an imaginative resemblance of the flower spurs to the talons of an eagle. The common name Columbine comes from *columba*, a dove; either avenue might lead to the speculation that this genus is for the birds. It should be noted, however, that the name is likely drawn from *aquilegis*, a water-finder, perhaps because many of the plants grow in moist soil near streams and lakes.

The wild European species, *A. vulgaris*, was grown in medieval days as a healing herb. It was used as a remedy for measles, small pox, and jaundice. It fell out of favour in medicine by the mid–eighteenth century. Linnaeus himself warned that he had known of overdoses that killed children.

Columbines remained a popular garden flower, often grown under the country name Granny Bonnets. Double forms were prized; Parkinson wrote, "The flowers hereof be very double, that is to say, many of those little flowers (having the forms of birds) are thrust one into the belly of another, sometimes blew, often white, and otherwhiles of mixt colours, as nature list to plaie with her little ones. . . ."

Chaucer and Shakespeare both mention columbines ("There's fennel for you, and columbines," says Ophelia in *Hamlet*), as did later and lesser writers. Victorian poetess Loisa Anne Twalmey found that, on account of the five tubular spurs, the columbine had been given the name Folly's Flower in allusion to the "the cap which Folly wears" in form of its nectary spurs, which turn over like the caps of jesters.

John Tradescant, Jr., sent seed of the first New World columbine discovered to his father, keeper of Charles I's gardens, in 1640. *A. canadensis* caused a mild shock with its yellow petals and red sepals, the red colouring extending into the backward-pointing spurs. The nodding blossoms dangle from airy stems from one to three feet tall. *A. canadensis* is the only species of *Aquilegia* indigenous to the eastern part of the United States, although its range extends as far west as Texas. It grows on rock ledges and cliffs in woodlands, hence the colloquial name Rock Bells. *A. formosa* inhabits western states and bears a close resemblance to *A. canadensis*; the pendant flowers, also red and yellow, truly warrant the name Jester's Cap.

Aquilegia caerulea
ROCKY MOUNTAIN COLUMBINE

Aquilegia canadensis
CANADIAN COLUMBINE

Aquilegia formosa
JESTER'S CAP

Aquilegia vulgaris
GRANNY BONNETS

The discovery of Rocky Mountain Columbine, *A. caerulea*, was a dividend of a government expedition led by Stephen Long in 1820 to explore the western portion of the Louisiana Purchase, particularly the source of the South Platte River, which they never found. Crossing the plains, which they called "The Great American Desert," the party was entranced by the sight of the Rockies, particularly the highest mountain, which would eventually become Longs Peak. They crossed the site of what was to become Denver and continued into the foothills. (Here they might have found the source of the Platte, had the party not gorged themselves on wild currants and become ill, abandoning their search just a few miles into Waterton Canyon.) Near Palmer Lake, the expedition's doctor and botanist Edwin James first came upon the long-spurred blue flower, hoping that "if it should appear not be have been described, it may receive the name of *Aquilegia caerulea*."

James has many firsts to his credit. The first botanist in Colorado, he was also the first white man to climb a mountain over 14,000 feet in North America. He departed with two companions from the main party to attempt a climb of Pikes Peak, and was overwhelmed by the "brilliantly flowering alpine plants" he found as he scaled the mountain, and collected many samples. Upon returning to their base camp, where they had neglected to douse the morning campfire, the men found the entire canyon in flames. James was also the state's first careless camper.

Armeria maritima
Plumbaginaceae

SEA PINK

When the practice of making knot gardens swept fashionable circles in Tudor times, the humble Sea Pink, *Armeria maritima*, was elevated to an esteemed status. "This is an everliving greene herbe," wrote Parkinson, "which many take to border their beds, and set their knots and trayles, and therein much delight, because it will grow thicke and bushie...." He further recommended Sea Pink for its summer display of "pleasant flowers, to decke up an house among other sweete herbes...."

Pliny the Elder (uncle of the younger Pliny) told that the plants were called *Statice*, meaning stop, as they held back the shifting beach sands. This name was later transferred to the closely related sea-lavenders, now called *Limonium*, and later to the everlasting flowers that have never seen a beach. *Armeria* was the Roman name for the genus *Dianthus* (to which they hold a superficial resemblance, if not close kinhood), and from their seaside origin, the plants came to be called Sea Pinks. Such is the logic of botany...

Armeria maritima is widely distributed in Europe, North Africa, and Asia. Though there are twenty distinct botanical varieties, they interbreed so freely that most botanists prefer not to recognize any as separate species. The plants form tufts of low-growing grassy leaves. They were sometimes called Ladies' Cushions, though they would make a suitable seat for only a very tiny lady. As one of the most variable flowers in cultivation, the foliage grows from four inches to a foot or more, and the flowers vary from deep pink to white.

The small individual flowers are held in bunches on stiff stems above the leaves.

As might be expected, Sea Pinks thrive best in well-drained sandy soil and benefit from a light winter mulch in cold winters. The grassy tufts are still employed for edging purposes and for knots. Rock gardeners depend on them for summer

Flower heads of *Armeria maritima* spill onto a gravel path, LEFT. A miniature bouquet, ABOVE, features Sea Pink, Partridge Feather, and Hattie's Pincushion.

colour, and they are similarly useful in perennial borders, planted in groups at the edge with Lamb's Ears and cranesbills.

No one seems to know the origin of the folk name Thrift for *A. maritima*, yet the flower was until recently represented on British threepenny bits. The name belies a generous production of flowers.

The milkweeds and silkweeds are indigenous to the New World. Native Americans used many of the one hundred or more species in healing, so the genus was named by botanists for Asklepios, the Greek god of medicine. The North American *Asclepias tuberosa* is among the most beautiful wildflowers. William Robinson called it "the prettiest species" of its genus, "with its clusters of showy bright orange-red flowers." Unlike most of its relatives, it has non-milky sap. Since Milkweed was out of the question, settlers dubbed it Silkweed for its beautiful tufts of hairs attached to its seeds. Jane Colden labelled it Silk Grass, from the seeds "crown'd with very long white Down." Butterflies flock to the umbels of brilliant orange flowers, hence Butterfly Weed.

The colonists added *A. tuberosa* to their list of simples as Pleurisy-root. A decoction from the roots was once widely used to treat chest complaints, such as asthma, bronchitis, and lung inflammations (pleurisy). The Native Americans of the Northeast called it "wound-medicine"; they pulverized dried roots and dusted the powder into cuts with a turkey feather.

Miss Colden, in her botanic manuscript of New York wild plants, related that, "The Root of this Asclepias taken in powder, is an exellent cure for the Colick, about halff a Spoonfull at a time. This cure was learn'd from a Canada Indian, & is calld in New England Canada Root." She also gives another recipe learned from the Native Americans: "One ounce of the Root, chiped into small pieces, to which put a pint & a halff of boiling water, & let it stew for about one hour, of this Decoction drinck halff a Tea cup full, every hour or two, and you bin certainly perfectly cured from the bloody Flux. . . ." It should be noted that Miss Colden's manuscript was written with a quilled pen and is a series of notes about particular plants. She was without the benefit of editors and proofreaders, who would surely have tidied up her Calamity Jane style.

Pleurisy-root was further employed as a laxative and diuretic, as well as for rheumatism and lameness. Gardeners today should be cautious about treating themselves with home remedies made from Butterfly Weed, for it can be toxic.

Luckily for the pioneers, however, *A. tuberosa* could be found in the wild from New Hampshire to Florida, and westward to the Rocky Mountains. It thrives in dry, sunny spots and is often found growing on

banks. Its long taproot enables Butterfly Weed to survive periods of drought, but makes transplanting an established plant a very risky business. New plants are easily grown from seed and take two or more years to begin flowering. Each root may send up as many as ten flowering stalks from one to three feet high, blooming from midsummer to early autumn. Both flowers and seed pods make startling additions to arrangements.

Asclepias tuberosa
Asclepiadaceae

BUTTERFLY WEED

A. tuberosa glows in summer, LEFT. Its silky seeds top a bouquet with Fleabane, Harebell, and Pearl Everlasting, ABOVE.

More than five hundred species of *Aster* are to be found, chiefly in North America, but also in Europe, Asia, and South America. The biggest splash was made when the showy species from New England landed in England. Several individual species with similar characteristics, notably *A. novae-angliae* and *A. novi-belgii*, are generally labelled Michaelmas Daisies. The feast day of St. Michael, known in England as Michaelmas, is celebrated on the last day of September, when the New World asters are conspicuously in bloom.

A. novi-belgii was first described by the German botanist Franz Hermann in 1687. He named it—in Latin, of course—for a little settlement where the seed had been collected. The town was New York, originally called New Amsterdam, but the English annexed the colony in 1664, renaming it to honour the Duke of York, later James II. The species is a variable one in both height and flower coloration. Purple, lavender, and white varieties grow in moist coastal regions from Newfoundland to Georgia. From one to six feet in height, New York Aster bears flowers with twenty to fifty thin petals, called ray-florets.

A. novae-angliae means simply New England Aster, although its range extends from open places in Vermont to moist meadows as far west as Wyoming and New Mexico. The flowers are from one to two inches across, and are crowded with as many as one hundred ray-florets. A rosy-purple tint is characteristic, and the leaves are considerably more hairy than those of their New York cousins.

Aster Compositae

Aster divaricatus
WHITE WOOD ASTER

Aster novae-angliae
MICHAELMAS DAISY

Aster novi-belgii
NEW YORK ASTER

Both species were introduced to English horticulture in 1710. With *A. laevis*, brought from America in 1758, selections and hybrids from these species comprise the bulk of garden selections of Michaelmas Daisies. Asters hybridize freely, much to the consternation of botanists. "Never was there so rascally a genus," declared Asa Gray; "they reduce me to despair."

Aster is Latin for star. The entire order of Compositae, of which the asters are members, is a family with upward of 9,000 species. They comprise the one-tenth of the floral kingdom that writer William Sutherland described in 1871 as "a horde of barbarians which no sane gardener would admit within the boundaries of the refined circles of the cultivated Flora."

Sanity is not a necessary attribute of a gardener, however. Space being a consideration, it is all the more telling of the beauty of the Michaelmas Daisies that so many good gardeners would devote so much room to them. Tinted photographs of Gertrude Jekyll's borders show masses of them, their lavender and purple colours that she dearly loved highlighted by silver and grey-leaved plants like *Stachys*, *Artemisia*, *Dianthus*, and *Phlomis*.

Five-foot *Rudbeckia triloba*, with its black-eyed brassy yellow flowers, makes a bolder companion for tall Michaelmas Daisies. Jewel-toned garden phloxes are equally effective counterparts. Taller-growing aster selections require sunny situations, regular irrigation, and plenty of elbow room. When in full bloom, a heavy rain is likely to cause them to flop; inconspicuous support can be devised. "Damned if the bees don't like it," commented a friend, surveying his six-foot specimen

smothered with lavender blossoms being industriously worked by hundreds of bees.

A good many asters besides the traditional Michaelmas Daisies have long been grown. The White Wood Aster, *A. divaricatus*, grows in woodlands from Quebec to Tennessee. The white-rayed flowers measure an inch across, and are held in loose, rounded clusters. The starry-white

Aster novi-belgii, OPPOSITE ABOVE, despite its name, has an extended range. Michaelmas Daisy glows in autumn, OPPOSITE BELOW. *A. divaricatus* makes a charming display in a terracotta pot with Black-eyed Susan, ABOVE.

display on two-foot stems is particularly effective in partial shade, enhanced by deepening shadows. *A. divaricatus* possesses a naturally relaxed posture that looks ridiculous staked into artificial rigidity. In the Jekyllian borders, it was planted behind bergenias, so that it could fall forward into the leathery leaves, surely a striking textural contrast.

Callirhoe involucrata Malvaceae

WINE CUP

Callirhoe was the daughter of Achelous, the river god of Greek mythology. She is chiefly remembered for her prayer to Zeus that her young sons grow to manhood in a single day (all mothers, no doubt, have days like this). In her case, the wish was granted so that they might avenge the murder of their father, which they did.

According to legend, another of her sons—Ganymede, who presumably did not grow as quickly—was abducted and taken to Mount Olympus. He became cupbearer of the gods—perhaps serving wine and ambrosia—and, eventually, immortal. Why this plant bears the name of his admittedly long-suffering mother, and not that of Ganymede, is open for question. Puzzling, too, is why a river god, presumably immortal, would not pass down immortality genes to his daughter and grandson, who had to earn immortality as a bartender? Achelous was not one of the really first-rate gods, having been defeated by Hercules in a struggle over the maiden Deianira, who, as Mrs. Hercules, unwittingly killed her husband by providing him with a shirt that had been dipped in poison blood. But Deianira's housekeeping is another story . . .

Wine Cup, *Callirhoe involucrata*, is a delightful perennial of the prairie with brilliant magenta-pink blossoms from May to September. The five-petalled beauties, two inches across, are chalice-shaped. The flower is sometimes misleadingly called Poppy Mallow, for it is neither poppy nor mallow, although it does belong to the Malvaceae. Early settlers on the plains dubbed it Buffalo Rose. The flowers bloom on sprawling stems up to two feet long. Its toothed leaves, resembling those of a maple, are deep grey-green.

A tribe of Native Americans, the Dakotas, smoked the dried, crushed roots of

C. involucrata is a gem of the American West, LEFT. Wine Cup blossoms tumble from a goblet in a niche, ABOVE.

C. involucrata to relieve head colds. The Dakota name for the plant, not surprisingly, translates as "smoke-treatment medicine." They drank a tea from the boiled roots for muscle aches.

Thomas Nuttall is credited with the discovery of *Callirhoe involucrata*, and for a time the genus was named *Nuttallia* in his honour. So too, was a genus that would end up as *Mentzelia*. The International Rules of Nomenclature, by which botanists and taxonomists must abide, works on a first come, first served basis. Because the plant had already been named by Asa Gray, Nuttall lost out.

Wine Cup grows in the wild from North Dakota and Missouri southward and westward to Texas and Utah. A long taproot contributes to its considerable drought tolerance, though it will grow well in most well-drained soils. Its flowers are particularly lovely seen tumbling down a stone wall or rock incline. In a flat border, Wine Cup can be paired with, and trained into, silver-foliaged plants such as Lamb's Ears, *Stachys byzantina*, or *Santolina chamaecyparissus*. The flowers appear particularly brilliant with these foils.

An equally showy perennial native of the southern states, *C. papaver* sports bright purplish-red flowers. So does two foot tall *C. digitata*, discovered in 1835 by Thomas Drummond in Texas, where he also found *Phlox drummondii*, an annual that would make his name a household word.

A sun-drenched site and dryish soil suit Wine Cup. Plants are relatively pest-free, and may be propagated by seed or cuttings. Care should be taken to disturb the roots as little as possible when transplanting this species.

There are but four species of the American genus *Chelone*, members of the family that also includes foxgloves and penstemons. They are segregated from penstemons by the two or three petal-like bracts at the base of their flowers. Gardeners, on the other hand, would support the separation of *Chelone* from the hundreds of *Penstemon* species by virtue of the shape of the flowers themselves. There is no denying that they are indeed reminiscent of the head of a turtle.

I kept a miraculous little turtle as a boy, the miracle being his escape from his bowl and a month long period during which, to my mother's horror, he was at large in the house. A large dust ball, swept from under my bed, proved to be my turtle, who revived after a good soak in his bowl. I did not see a species of Turtle-head until some twenty years later, but the flowers stirred memories of the episode, which I had totally forgotten.

Chelone is simply Greek for turtle, and should be pronounced to sound something like Key-low-nay. Appropriately, Turtle-heads are moisture-loving perennials inhabiting moist woodlands. *C. obliqua* is

A handsome colony of Turtle-head, RIGHT, is bordered by a drift of Cupid's Dart, *Catananche caerulea*.

Chelone obliqua Scrophulariaceae

TURTLE-HEAD

found from Maryland to Arkansas, as far north as Minnesota and as far south as Alabama. It is distinguished by bright pink flowers, up to an inch and a half long, set on upright stems growing to three feet or higher. Deep green leaves enhance the pink flowers that bloom in July and into the autumn. Jane Colden described closely related *C. glabra* in New York about 1750 with the notation that the flower was like "a bellied Pipe, the under side of it flat . . . large and white, only that the Lips are of a redish colour. . . ."

Folk medicine employed Turtle-head to treat jaundice, fever, ulcers, and herpes. A tea was brewed from the leaves to stimulate the appetite and to expel worms, but presumably not simultaneously. It was also called Shell-flower and Balmony. The flowers are as undervalued today as they were in 1890, when Peter Henderson wrote of their "singular beauty entitling them to a place in every collection."

Turtle-head thrives in partially shaded areas where abundant moisture is available, and looks especially pleasing in waterside plantings. *C. obliqua* is easily propagated by division, cuttings, or from seed. Once established, clumps are of the easiest culture, requiring nothing but a spring clean-up from the gardener.

The flower heads of *Chelone obliqua*, LEFT, bear an uncanny resemblance (except in colour) to those of turtles.

A PORTFOLIO OF ANTIQUE SPECIES

Feverfew is native to southeastern Europe, but has taken up residence in Britain and parts of North America. The ancients called it *febrifugia*, Latin for "a substance that drives out fevers." The name stuck. Feverfew may be one of the few flowers which is almost universally recognized by its common name, rather than a scientific one which seems to change as regularly as the Palace Guard.

This plant was first called *Parthenium* by early botanists, because a story was told by Plutarch in *The Life of Pericles* of a worker who fell during the construction of the Parthenon whose life was saved by the plant. The plant is familiar to many gardeners, but not under the many names assigned to it over the years. It has variously been transferred from genus to genus as a *Matricaria*, *Pyrethrum*, and most recently, as *Tanacetum*, but it is still generally known as *Chrysanthemum parthenium*.

Aside from its value in reducing fevers, the plant had other uses. Gerard claimed Feverfew was "very good for them that are giddie in the head, or which have the turning called Vertigo. . . ." (he, too, had heard of the giddie Greek toppling off the Parthenon), and mentioned that "also it is good for such as be melancholike, sad, pensive and without speech." Parkinson described it as "a special remedy to helpe those that have taken Opium too liberally." A tea brewed from the flowers, mixed with nutmeg and wine, and drunk throughout the day, was said to relieve women of nervous conditions (highly likely), to treat colds, expel worms, and help women to become pregnant.

The flowers resemble small daisies with very short rays, and are displayed in loose clusters on branched stems growing up to three feet. A double form, 'Flore-pleno,' looking like plump little pompoms, was popular in England as early as 1600. The pinnate leaves of Feverfew, much like autumn garden "mums," are highly aromatic. A form with golden leaves, 'Aureum,' was esteemed by the Victorians and used extensively in geometric floral plantings. Feverfew, occasionally called Featherfew as well, was among the invaluable medicinal plants grown from the first by American colonists. Fifty years after the Pilgrims landed on Plymouth Rock, an English gentleman, John Josselyn, published a book based on eight years of study in the New World. In it was a "list of such garden Herbs (amongst us) as do thrive there and such as do not." Although he noted that "Southernwood is no plant for this Country, Nor Rosemary," he proclaimed that, "Featherfew prospereth exceedingly."

There is hardly as pretty a flower so eager to grow in gardens. Sun or part-shade are fine, and it will thrive in stiff clay or sandy soils as long as it has some water. Feverfew survives cold winters, although old woody plants may succumb. Replacements are never a problem with a myriad of self-sown seedlings; wags dub it Feverplenty. It may be naturalized in wild gardens. If cut back after the first flush of

Chrysanthemum balsamita
COSTMARY

Chrysanthemum leucanthemum
OX-EYE DAISY

Chrysanthemum parthenium
FEVERFEW

The double form of Feverfew, LEFT, glistens against hedges. Ox-eye Daisy, TOP, is often called Measure-of-love. The flowers of Costmary, ABOVE, bloom with herbs.

Chrysanthemum Compositae

bloom in June and July, it often repeats later. The flowers are particularly valuable in all-white schemes. They are a lovely and long-lasting addition to bouquets.

Modern research has discovered the leaves may be valuable in treating those with chronic migraines. Experiments at Chelsea College in London found that eating one to five fresh leaves per day was beneficial for sufferers. Buoyed by that news, my neighbour has taken to drinking Feverfew tea for her headaches, although the taste of the leaves is unbelievably bitter. Bees rarely, if ever, frequent the flowers—they, too, are put off by the bitter taste. Sprigs of flowers poked in a buttonhole may keep bees away while working in the garden. Insects in general avoid Feverfew.

Another species, *C. balsamita*, is commonly called Costmary or Alecost as it was used to flavour mulled ale. Costmary may come from the old Latin name *costus amarus*, meaning an aromatic and bitter shrub, although it may also refer to St. Mary, with whom the plant was connected in medieval days. The designation *balsamita* implies the aroma of Balsam, and it was grown in England for the fragrant leaves as early as the fourteenth century. It originated in western Asia, but can be found wild now in parts of the United States, a relic from colonial gardens. Some taxonomists reclassify *C. balsamita* as *Balsamita major*; gardeners generally ignore the new name.

The golden yellow disc flowers, with a resemblance to Feverfew's, lack ray-florets, meaning they are without petals. The oblong basal leaves are often ten inches long. They have a pleasant, sweet odour, and colonists pressed them into service as bookmarks; hence the nickname Bible Leaf. The shape of the leaves led some to call it Goose Tongue. The plant also has a bitter taste, but one variety has a strong flavour of spearmint, and was known as Mint Geranium. The leaves were added to salads and other foods for seasoning. As a stuffing for veal, it was known as Sage of Bedlam, probably corrupted from Bethlehem.

The culture is similar to that of Feverfew, although full sun is preferable to prevent straggly flower stems, which usually grow to three or four feet, and, like Feverfew, it is virtually immune from insects. (I hasten to note that slugs are not insects.)

The Ox-eye Daisy, *C. leucanthemum*, grows wild throughout Europe and in North America, where it immigrated to with early colonists. The plant is sometimes classified under the name *Leucanthemum vulgare*, but gardeners resist the change. Margaret of Anjou, wife of Henry VI, took three daisies as her heraldic symbol, embroidering them on her robes and those of her courtiers. The flower is often called Marguerite in her honour, as well as for six saints with the same name. St. Margaret of the Dragon was driven from Antioch by her father, a heathen priest, when she would not renounce the Christian faith. (Somewhere along the line, she also slew a dragon.) In her prayers she held her face toward heaven like a daisy, it was said.

In myth, the daisy was once a sprightly dryad seen dancing on the green by Vertumnus, god of spring. Smitten with passion, he lunged for the delicate white creature. With fear and aversion in her "eye," and with divine aid, she sank to the ground in the form of a daisy.

Quaint folk names for *C. leucanthemum* include Trembling Star in Wales, Easter Flower in France, and Goose Flower in Germany. It is also called A-thousand-charms, Meadow Pearl, Whiteweed, and Measure-of-love, from the timeless maidenly custom of pulling off its petals to discover if "he loves me" or "loves me not." Untold numbers of daisies have been shredded over hundreds of years by countless girls until they got the right answer.

Ribbons won by champion bulls, ABOVE, highlight clusters of single Feverfew flowers. Ox-eye Daisy is dwarfed by an ancient Minoan storage jar from Crete, OPPOSITE; the pairing underscores tales of the flowers' mythological origins.

Cimicifuga is derived from the Latin words, *cimex*, a bug, and *fugare*, to drive away, in reference to an Asian custom of burning some species of the plant to repel insects. One common name, Bugbane, stems from the practice, although it is inappropriate for the American kinds, which provided no such service. Furthermore, the name carries a rather unappealing association, not-at-all the stuff of poetry:

O'er the wooded land and down the country lane
Drat mosquitos chased us 'til we spied Bugbane.

(As the poet, I prefer anonymity.)

Colonists found *C. racemosa* growing wild in forests from Massachusetts to Ohio, as far south as Tennessee. It was called Black Cohosh, a name probably derived from a Native American one. The medicinal roots are dark in colour. John Bartram, who could never pass up a pretty plant, brought *C. racemosa* into his garden in Pennsylvania. He is credited with sending the first seeds to his friend Peter Collinson in England about 1760.

Black Snakeroot's long medicine tradition passed from Native Americans to settlers, who fought fevers, lumbago, rheumatism, chorea, and snakebites with a tincture from the roots. It was used to aid in childbirth, and was important in treating all manner of female complaints. The colloquial name Squaw Root refers to these applications. Modern science has successfully strengthened the reproductive processes of female rats with root extracts from *C. racemosa*, though one wonders whether this enhancement is necessary or advisable.

Coarse-toothed leaves, usually once- or twice-divided, form handsome clumps. From these arise tall spires of flowers, six feet or taller, in midsummer. The slender racemes are composed of hundreds of creamy white flowers, each with a tuft of protruding stamens, giving a bottle-brush appearance. Viewed in a sylvan setting, the folk name Fairy Candles seems a fitting one for the tapering spires.

C. racemosa performs best in light shade, especially in warm climates, but it will grow well in any situation where it is planted in rich, organic soil and watered well. Root cuttings or division are the best ways to increase stock, but plants take several years to reach their peak. The dramatic flower spikes tower gracefully over traditional perennials in a border, or make effective accents in wooded gardens among ferns, hostas, and rhododendrons. The flowers are rarely, if ever, to be found in the cut flower trade, but arrangers have a field day with home-grown stems. The plants of Black Snakeroot are nearly bug-free.

BLACK SNAKEROOT

*Spires of *Cimicifuga racemosa*, LEFT, make ethereal companions for Gold-banded Lily, *Lilium auratum*. An arrangement with *C. racemosa* springs from an antique wellhead, ABOVE.*

Cimicifuga racemosa
Ranunculaceae

A PORTFOLIO OF ANTIQUE SPECIES

Coreopsis is from the Greek *koris*, a bug, and *opsis*, indicating resemblance. In short, the seeds look like bugs—namely, ticks. Why such a pretty flower should be cursed with such an unappealing common name as Tickseed is as unfathomable as the rather unhealthy obsession by so many botanists with insects.

I fear too many gardeners may view Tickseed as unwholesome, and may harbour a fear of spreading Rocky Mountain Spotted Fever if they planted it. The bright daisy flowers of the genus *Coreopsis* might have inspired a fanciful name—perhaps for Apollo, the sun god—but instead are named for their unremarkable seeds. "Rhinoseed" would certainly make me sit up and take notice, but I am not in the least interested in ticks, unless I find them in my hair.

One of the first of this exclusively American genus to be introduced to England was *C. lanceolata* about 1725. Early colonists found the golden daisy-like blossoms, often more than two inches across, in many areas. Sunny meadows from Michigan to Florida, as far west as New Mexico, glowed with the flowers throughout the summer. A very similar species, *C. grandiflora*, is indigenous to the southern plains. Double-flowered selections of these two species, which grow from one to three feet in height, are perennial favourites.

Perennial *C. verticillata* was introduced to English gardens in 1823. Found growing wild on the savannas from Maryland to Georgia, the thin-petalled, golden-yellow

flowers are smaller than those of *C. lanceolata*, but they are produced in abundance. They are held on upright stems clad with finely cut leaves; the binomial *verticillata* recognizes their whorled appearance.

Nuttall discovered *C. tinctoria* in Arkansas about 1820, and it arrived shortly thereafter in England. The two-toned annual, usually with sienna red petals shading to yellow tips, was an immediate hit with British gardeners. Its rapid spread from one garden to another led Benajmin Maund to remark at the time, "In the three years since the period of its introduction, its beauty has secured it a passport to almost every respectable garden in the kingdom."

The flowers of the plains wildflower were used by Native Americans to dye cloth red; *tinctoria* means to be used in dyeing. In addition, the roots were used by the tribes of the prairie to treat diarrhoea and as an emetic to induce vomiting. *C. tinctoria* is common in grasslands throughout the Midwest, and has escaped from cultivation in some states, further extending its range both east and west. It flourishes with little care, growing from a spring sowing to three feet or more, and flowering all summer and into autumn. The plants are reliable "volunteers" in following years. Selected strains feature colour and pattern variations, as well as dwarf habits.

The species was, for a time, awarded its own genus, *Calliopsis*, meaning beautiful eye. This disallowed name from the nineteenth century is still to be found in a few catalogues, perhaps because some seed merchants stalwartly resist calling it Tickseed again.

Coreopsis Compositae

Thin leaves identify *C. verticillata*, LEFT. *C. tinctoria*, BELOW, was once called Nuttall's Weed. ILLUSTRATION, *C. lanceolata*.

Coreopsis lanceolata
TICKSEED

Coreopsis tinctoria
CALLIOPSIS

Coreopsis verticillata
THREAD-LEAF
COREOPSIS

A PORTFOLIO OF ANTIQUE SPECIES

Daucus carota Umbelliferae

QUEEN ANNE'S LACE

76 Wild Flowers

Queen Anne's Lace, a wildflower of romance and imagery, is nothing more than a carrot, *Daucus carota*. The cultivated garden vegetable differs not a whit, botanically, from the wildling so common in fields of New England.

In Elizabethan England, there was very little difference even in the looks of the domesticated and wild carrot that are native to the Mediterranean region. Carrots had not yet been plumped up to Bugs Bunny size, but they were consumed, if not esteemed. The root was "commonly boiled with fat flesh and eaten," according to Gerard. "The nourishment," he noted, "is not much, and not verie good . . . something windie, but not so much as be the Turnips. . . ."

Wild carrot, on the other hand, held a reputation as something of an aphrodisiac. Pliny the Elder quoted Orpheus in contending that it "winneth love." It contained "a certain force to procure lust." Boiled in wine, the roots were believed to "helpeth conception." Even Gerard subscribed to this theory. It could also be mixed with honey to cleanse running sores and taken to expel kidney stones. None of the herbalists, curiously, mention that it could strengthen eyesight.

The English called the wild form Bird's Nest, an apt description of the flower head. It has long been held that sentimental American colonists most likely coined Queen Anne's Lace, a tribute to the monarch, last of the Stuarts, famous for her elaborate skill with a needle. The name, however, can be traced to Anne of Denmark, wife of James I. The pretty blonde queen loved fine clothes and jewelry, and portraits of her show fine lace at her wrists, bodice, and collar. A court observer described Anne and her ladies "like so many nymphs or nereides," apparently all arrayed in ivory lace, "to the ravishment of the beholders." It is not entirely clear which queen is honoured by Queen Anne's Jonquil, Queen Anne's Thimble, or Queen Anne's Pocket Melon.

The Dutch first began to select the culinary carrots in the fifteenth century. The Puritans brought both the wild and domestic varieties to the New World, one for healing, the other for the stew pot. Carrots are biennial plants, forming rosettes of ferny leaves the first season, and they bloom, set seed, and die the next. The flower umbels are composed of up to 2,500 tiny florets. The flowers attract all manner of bees, butterflies, and beetles to pollinate them, and it is not unusual for one flower head to release 4,000 seeds. The wild ones colonized the New World even more quickly than the human immigrants. The common roadside weeds, such a part of New England's summer pleasures, charm farmers considerably less; some call them the Devil's Plague.

Few New Englanders bother to cultivate Queen Anne's Lace in their gardens, since a bouquet can be picked just down the road, even along expressways in New York City when rush hour traffic comes to a standstill. Gardeners in other parts of the country, especially in the West, delight in introducing the antique lace of *D. carota* to irrigated borders. Here too, it will naturalize itself with romantic abandon.

D. carota blooms seaside with Goldenrod, LEFT, and with Evening Primrose, ABOVE.

A PORTFOLIO OF ANTIQUE SPECIES 77

PURPLE CONEFLOWER

Echinacea purpurea combines prettily with Larkspur, Garden Phlox, and Acidanthera bicolor, BELOW. The flowers are backed by *Salvia sclarea,* RIGHT.

Whimsically minded gardeners enjoy the derivation of the name *Echinacea purpurea*, which, thankfully, has nothing to do with bugs. *Echinos* is Greek for hedgehog, while *purpurea* means purple. Purple hedgehog is a fair description of the flower, a prickly centre cone ringed by purplish pink ray-florets. Gardeners commonly use the misleading name Purple Coneflower, although the flowers fall more into the pink part of the spectrum. American pioneers coined the quaint names Red Sunbonnet and Ozark Droops, alluding to the drooping ray-florets of these daisies.

John Banister, an employee of the Bishop of London, Henry Compton, was sent to Virginia to observe and collect American plants for the horticulturally minded bishop. Seed of the perennial reached Compton, as well as the Oxford Botanic Garden, by 1690. It was originally classified by Linnaeus in 1754 as a *Rudbeckia*, but technical differences in the structure of its cylindrical centres warranted the creation of a new genus in 1794. Purple Coneflower has remained a garden favourite from the time of its introduction, except during the Victorian bedding craze, when it was considered too tall and too uninhibited to be of garden value.

Perhaps this untamed quality accounts for the affection so many gardeners, myself included, hold for it today. *E. purpurea* is native to open woodlands and prairies from Georgia to Oklahoma, as far north as Michigan, and south to Louisiana. The stout stems grow from three to five feet, and the simple toothed leaves are deep ol-

ive green. Fine bristly hairs cover the stems and foliage. The flower heads measure up to six inches in diameter. They are crowned in the centre by a dark brown cone, green in the interior, from which protrude the conspicuous orange bracts.

This hedgehog disc is set off by the dozen or more petals, or ray-florets. The intensity of their coloration is variable in wild populations, but is often wine-pink with a pale violet cast. Cultivated varieties range in colour from mauve-crimson to white. Interestingly, the petals do not fall as they fade, but curl and dry on the heads. The dried flower heads were used by women of the Kiowa and Meskwaki to comb their hair, hence the not-very-common name Comb Plant.

Native Americans of the plains used Purple Coneflower more than any other medicinal plant. The roots were used to treat a litany of ailments and accidents, including bites of snakes and spiders, burns, sores, toothaches, and flu. Pharmaceutical preparations from *E. purpurea* and other *Echinacea* species, including *E. pallida*, are to this day made in Europe, especially in Germany. Modern research confirms the validity of many traditional uses, especially in treating allergies and viral infections.

Garden uses are as varied as medicinal ones. Purple Coneflower, which may be easily grown from seed, thrives in full sun or with a bit of shade. It grows best in sandy loam, although it tolerates diverse conditions and is somewhat tolerant of drought. The flowers, produced in midsummer and sometimes into autumn, are pleasing with all flowers and foliage in the cool part of the spectrum. A backdrop of silver artemisias is highly effective. Purple Coneflower is a bold, if not an elegant plant, so fine-textured blue flowers—centaureas, larkspurs, and nigellas—further enhance the flowers of Purple Coneflower. Its charm is undeniable in any garden combination or bouquet.

Echinacea purpurea Compositae

 A few wildflowers that bloom in both North America and Europe are not immigrants from one country to another, but rather, they are truly indigenous to both worlds. Scottish Bluebell and American Harebell are one and the same, *Campanula rotundifolia*. Cow Parsnip, *Heracleum sphondylium*, is native to northern Europe, Siberia, Canada, and the United States as far south as Georgia. Another such survivor of the days before the land bridge between Alaska and Siberia sank beneath the sea is *Epilobium angustifolium*.

The scientific name is derived from the Greek *epi*, upon, and *lobos*, a pod, in allusion to the placement of the flowers. Some experts classify the plant as *Chamaenerion angustifolium*, but *Epilobium* remains in common use. The English call it Willow Herb, while Americans prefer Fireweed. Both have merit. In the Old World, an ale was brewed from the dried pith, the tender young shoots were cooked much like asparagus, and stockings were made from a cloth woven from cotton and the down from the seed heads. The dried leaves were added to tea blends to imitate the flavour of China tea.

Gerard described it as "having leaves like the greatest Willow . . . garnished with brave flowers of great beautie, consisting of fower leaves a peece, of an orient purple colour . . . which do grow in my garden very goodly to behold." Folk names for *E. angustifolium*—the specific epithet means narrow-leaved—included French Willow, Rose Bay, and Blooming Sally. The flower was so rare in seventeenth-century England that Parkinson was not aware that it was a native. "Wee have not knowne where this willowe floure groweth naturally," he wrote, "but we have it standing in an out-corner of our Gardens, to fill up the number of delightfull flowers."

E. angustifolium is among the first of wildflowers to re-vegetate scorched land after a forest fire. The seeds can lay dormant for years, the seedlings emerging from the ashes to take advantage of the abundant sunshine after the trees have been destroyed. Londoners similarly were cheered by the sight of the bright flowers blooming in the rubble from bombings. What was once a rather uncommon wildflower has profited from the devastation of two world wars, as well as the construction of modern highways and timber cutting, to expand its range.

Some say it is too opportunistic, and as it proliferates by self-sown seedlings and a running rootstock, it is often too weedy

Epilobium angustifolium Onagraceae

WILLOW HERB

for a refined garden. Still, there are situations where it has enormous appeal. The flowers are borne in spires on three- to six-foot stems; the single blossoms, about an inch across, have the texture of poppies, and glow in rich magenta-pink or white. Flowers of considerably less charm by far are welcomed to gardens.

The old trick of planting mint in a bottomless bucket sunk into the soil to curb its wanderlust can be similarly employed for Willow Herb. I take no such precautions, instead pitting the plant against equally formidable opponents—Japanese Anemone, Old Gooseneck, *Lysimachia clethroides*, and Obedience, *Physostegia virginiana*. I have no wish to be without any of them, so I let them fight it out in the border, far removed from the primroses one would not want to throw to these wolves. A gardener who is not conscientious about removing the seeds may deride *E. angustifolium* for its invasiveness.

"The Garden does not afford a Plant more specious and elegant than this," proclaimed English writer John Hill in the mid–eighteenth century, ". . . and those who have Judgement despise the little Prejudices which represent every Thing as mean that comes easily." I must heartily concur, for if I am to be invaded, let it be by lovely Willow Herb.

Young shoots of *Epilobium angustifolium*, LEFT, have long been eaten—either boiled or soaked in seal oil—by the Eskimos, who called the dish *pahmeyuktuk*. ILLUSTRATION, a close-up of the blossom reveals four satiny petals.

PORTFOLIO OF ANTIQUE SPECIES 81

The genus *Eupatorium* is enormous, with more than a thousand species. Most are centred on Mexico and South America, as well as the West Indies. A few are indigenous to North America, Asia, and Europe. The name *Eupatorium* honours Mithridates Eupator, the king of ancient Pontus, a country bordering on the Black Sea, who is credited with the discovery that one kind was an antidote to poison. It seems that Mithridates, who ruled in the first century B.C., was the target of many attempts on his life through poisoning. Realizing that he was not universally admired by his subjects, he gradually immunized himself to every poison known by taking gradually increasing doses. His hobby was dabbling in antidotes, just to be on the safe side.

The most famous of the genus, *E. purpureum*, was a prominent healing plant of the New England Indians. It came to be called Joe Pye Weed, after the nineteenth-century medicine showman who promoted the root to induce sweating in typhus fever. Contrary to popular opinion, Pye was Caucasian, not an authentic medicine man.

Joe Pye Weed grows in thickets from New Hampshire to Florida, and west to Nebraska. It became a traditional medicinal herb to treat gout, urinary ailments, asthma, fevers, chills, and impotence. Several related species are often called by the common name, but *E. purpureum* is the most widely grown. Thriving in moist, sunny meadows, it can reach a dizzying twelve feet in height. Fortunately for the gardener, it rarely does so, and its growth can be somewhat controlled by the amount of irrigation it receives and by midseason pinching. The flowers are held in tight, round clusters from July into early autumn. Not the standard daisy-type blossoms of the Compositae, the fuzzy, pale rose-purple flowers most closely resemble those of *Ageratum*, to which they are closely related.

E. rugosum, native from Quebec to Louisiana, is a striking autumn-blooming species with white flowers. It carries the folk names White Snakeroot and Boneset. John Winthrop, the first governor of the Massachusetts Bay Colony, considered it wise to always have a bit of snakeroot when travelling about the countryside. The roots were dug and dried for treating snakebites and for other medicinal purposes.

It was much later that gardeners came to value the flowers of both species for their beauty and ease of culture. Both are trouble free, hardy perennials that may add a soft, pastel touch to traditional borders or naturalistic gardens.

Eupatorium purpureum
JOE PYE WEED

Eupatorium rugosum
WHITE SNAKEROOT

Eupatorium
Compositae

Eupatorium purpureum colours a moist meadow in summer and autumn with its clusters of fluffy flowers, OPPOSITE and ABOVE. ILLUSTRATION, The white flowers of *E. rugosum* bear a close resemblance to those of its purple cousin, *E. purpureum*.

Gaillardia Compositae

Gaillardia aristata FIREWHEEL

Gaillardia pulchella INDIAN BLANKET

Ray-florets of Firewheel, ABOVE, are boldly painted. Quilled forms of
G. pulchella, RIGHT, were bred more than a century ago.

The first *Gaillardia* to arrive in Europe was *G. pulchella* about 1780. The name commemorates M. Gaillard de Charentonneau, a French magistrate and patron of botany. We may thank the bestower of the name for his foresight in not tagging the genus with Gaillard's entire surname.

G. pulchella is most often grown as an annual, but may behave as a perennial in its extensive home range from Virginia to Florida, and westward throughout the prairie states. It grows from one to two feet in height, and the flowers measure two inches across. The flat petals, or rayflorets, may be yellow or bicolored, but are most often a maroon red. Willa Cather spoke of them blooming in Nebraska meadows "matted over the ground with the deep velvety red that is in Bokhara carpets." The country name Blanket Flower evokes a similar picture of the blossoms covering the plains.

German horticulturists selected seed strains for particular colours and patterns, and in 1881 achieved the variety 'Lorenziana', which is distinguished by quilled, tubular petals. This frothy form blooms in varying shades, and resembles a lollipop pulled from a child's pocket, all covered with lint.

The perennial *G. aristata*, native from Colorado to British Columbia, was discovered during the Lewis and Clark expedition. The plants grow to two or three feet in height, and are characterized by the sage green leaves and stems, both of which wear a fine coat of hairs. The flowers measure as much as four inches across, with a dark centre disc. The petals are typically corn yellow with a contrasting pattern of maroon toward the centre. One particularly evocative folk name from the West is Firewheel.

The two species met in a Belgian nursery in 1857, and the resulting spontaneous progeny were to set gardens ablaze with their gold and blood red flowers. These hybrids, properly *G. × grandiflora*, behave as perennials and have become valued ornamentals. The flowers display zigzag patterns as varied as an Indian Blanket, by which name they are also called.

Indian Blankets grow best in porous, even rubbly, free-draining soil. They tend to succumb over the winter if the roots rot in saturated clay. A sunny site is preferred, where they will bloom over a very long period from June into autumn, especially if the spent flowers are not allowed to set seed. *G. pulchella*—*pulchella* means pretty in Latin—may be started ahead of time in the greenhouse, or sown directly in the garden, where they will bloom on wiry stems perfect for arranging.

Graham Stuart Thomas says, "The flowers are admirable for cutting and give 'point' to many a vase of flowers." The gardener would find it pointless to argue.

Gaura is taken from the Greek *gauros*, meaning proud or superb. To read what some English writers have said about *G. lindheimeri*, one would suspect it was misnamed. But talk to a Texan gardener, and the story is quite different. What flops and fails to impress in the British Isles is a galloping success throughout much of the United States. (To be fair, I must point out that Beth Chatto, whose garden in summer is drier and warmer than the British norm, speaks highly of its performance.)

The handsome perennial was discovered about 1850 by Ferdinand Lindheimer, a botanical collector in the Southwest for John Torrey and Asa Gray. Boston horticulturist Joseph Breck praised the new introduction, calling *G. lindheimeri* "one of the finest we have received," as well as "fine for bouquets." He thought it was just fine. But because of its failure to adapt to rich living in Europe, *G. lindheimeri* never got the English stamp of approval.

The slender stems of *G. lindheimeri* rise from a basal clump of dark-green leaves. The foliage is often spotted with red patches; this is no cause for alarm and is quite natural. The ethereal flowers, about three-quarters of an inch across, open white and take on a pink blush as they age. The flowers have four petals, and a long fluff of stamens. They look like apple blossoms that have lost a petal or two in the wind. The name Apple-blossom Grass describes the wands of flowers swaying in the breeze. It is also called Wild Honeysuckle and Bee Blossom.

The plants have an airy grace, and are recommended by a long season of bloom. A huge swath of them in my garden blooms from June to October, the display becoming prettier by the month. They thrive with little attention and modest irrigation in a sunny position, and tolerate almost any type of soil. The stems grow to four feet in height, but some gardeners keep them more tightly in bounds with a spring pruning to promote shorter, bushier growth. It is best propagated by seed—it will often do this itself—and should be transplanted carefully so as not to injure the long taproot. Mature plants are difficult to move. Though the plants are hardy in many cold climates—the limits are still being tested—it may be grown quite successfully as an annual, as Breck suggested more than a century ago.

Apple-blossom Grass appeals to gardeners who appreciate its willowy grace. The blooming stems combine effortlessly with more substantial round or spiked flowers, both in the garden and in bouquets, such as malvas, zinnias, and salvias.

Gaura lindheimeri
Onagraceae

APPLE-BLOSSOM GRASS

An airy bouquet, OPPOSITE, holds *Gaura lindheimeri*, Cupid's Dart, Mealycup Sage, and Sea Lavender. *G. lindheimeri* dances in a breeze, ABOVE and BELOW.

Once, according to tall tales, every gentian was closed. Three fairies, caught in the rain late one evening (no doubt stumbling home from a wee folks night out on the woods) came upon three gentian flowers. The fairies begged the flowers to open up and allow them haven from the elements. The flowers refused (knowing the reputation of fairies, who can blame them?). The wet fairies travelled until they came to three more gentians, whom they finally persuaded to allow their buds to be used as motels for the evening. The grateful fairies left a gift in the morning: the flowers remained open, revealing their inner beauty.

Thus we may assume that the first three flowers were those of *Gentiana clausa*, the Closed Gentian. Native to damp woodlands from Maine to North Carolina, it grows from one to two feet tall. The unbranched stems terminate in a cluster of violet-blue flowers in late summer. The individual flowers are up to an inch and a half in length and are flask-shaped, as the folk name Bottle Gentian suggests. The plump flowers appear to be on the verge of opening at any moment, but never do. Pollination is accomplished by determined bumblebees that part the closed petal lips to tunnel inside. Getting out is no easy task either; occasionally a flower will shake violently from a claustrophobic customer trying to find the exit.

Gentiana clausa
Gentianaceae

CLOSED GENTIAN

Bumblebees must fight to enter the perpetually-closed flowers of *Gentiana clausa*, ABOVE, to reach the nectar. Closed Gentian grows best in partial shade, RIGHT.

G. clausa and the similar *G. andrewsii* are of much easier culture than many of the classic alpine gentians from Europe. They thrive in organically rich soil with abundant moisture. They are ideal companions for other flowers of the New England countryside, such as pink Turtle-head, Cardinal Flower, or Joe Pye Weed, which similarly revel at pond side or in moist borders. Appalachian settlers once employed the roots to treat snake bites.

The genus is named for King Gentius of Illyria (an ancient country bordering the Adriatic Sea), who in the second century B.C. was said to have discovered the healing properties of the yellow-flowering European species, *G. lutea*. This claim is disputed by the Hungarians, who assert one of their kings, Ladislaus, discovered the medicinal powers of gentian roots in 1087. He shot an arrow, so the story goes, with a prayer that it might reveal a cure for a terrible sickness ravaging his troops (who, in turn, were supposed to be ravaging Croatia). The arrow stuck in a gentian root, and the soldiers were not only cured, but were filled with such zeal that they conquered Slovenia as well. Ladislaus promptly became a saint.

Botany makes strange bedfellows. *Gillenia* is a member of the Rose family; most gardeners might wonder if some mistake hasn't been made. Nevertheless, the tiny, two-member genus is of the Rosaceae for scientific reasons of reproduction, not cosmetic ones. The name commemorates Arnold Gillen, a seventeenth-century German doctor and naturalist. It was introduced to England in 1713, at which point it was classified as *Spiraea trifoliata*. An attempt has been made to change the current name to *Porteranthus*, but the horticultural world has been dragging its collective heels.

G. trifoliata earns its specific epithet from its attractive leaves, divided into three leaflets. The wiry stems grow three or four feet high, topped by loose panicles of white flowers in early summer. The blossoms have five thin petals with a touch of red where they converge in the center. The red calyces persist after the petals have dropped. Individual flowers are less than an inch across, but are produced so freely as to appear, from a distance, like foam. I am tempted to describe the effect as dainty—a word that is just barely part of my vocabulary—so perhaps it is best to quote William Robinson's succinct appraisal in *The English Flower Garden* (1883) as "distinct and graceful."

Bowman's Root, *G. trifoliata* occurs in upland woods throughout the eastern part of North America. The only other relative, smaller- and later-blooming *G. stipulata*, is known colloquially as American-ipecac, by which name it has not secured passage into very many gardens. Both species are known as Indian Physic. A tea brewed from the leaves or roots was strongly laxative and emetic. Other traditional uses included small doses for indigestion, colds, and coughs. A poultice of the plant was applied for stings and insect bites.

Bowman's Root is a hardy perennial that offers no great cultural challenges. It grows best in partial shade, planted in rich loam and watered regularly. It is tolerant of less-than-ideal situations. New plants may be had from division or seed. Its flowering coincides with some of the stellar attractions of the June border, for which it makes an ideal companion. Peony and clematis flowers are stunning surrounded by the tiny star-like blooms of *G. trifoliata* —something like the way bouquets of roses used to look with a spray of Baby's-breath. This was before too many florists stuffed in too much of the filler, and the pairing was outlawed by the International Congress of Floral Disapproval (held in someone's living room about 1953).

BOWMAN'S ROOT

A garden tapestry, RIGHT, features a froth of the white flowers of *Gillenia trifoliata* encircling hybrid Clematis.

Gillenia trifoliata Rosaceae

Glaucium flavum
Papaveraceae

HORNED POPPY

The satiny flowers of the Horned Poppy recall its close kinship with the annual and perennial poppies so beloved in gardens. The genus *Glaucium* is a distinct one, however; the word is derived from the Greek *glaukos*, referring to the grey-blue leaves. In Greek mythology, Glaucus was the son of Neptune and a sea nymph. He chose to live on land, but spent his hours fishing on the shore. After landing a particularly big catch, the fish wriggled to a yellow poppy growing in the sand, ate the leaves, and with renewed strength, leapt back into the sea. Intrigued, Glaucus nibbled on the leaves of the poppy himself. He felt himself inexplicably drawn to the waves, dived into the sea, and "by transmutation strange" became a sea god. The silvery-leaved plant is often found growing near the sea. Robert Bridges (1844–1930) captured, with his pen, the age-old mystique of the Horned Poppy:

> *A poppy grows upon the shore,*
> *Burst her twin cups in summer late:*
> *Her leaves are glaucous-green and hoar,*
> *Her petals yellow, delicate . . .*
>
> *She has no lovers like the red,*
> *That dances with the noble corn:*
> *Her blossoms on the waves are shed,*
> *Where she stands shivering and forlorn.*

The most conspicuous feature of the Horned Poppy is its elongated seed capsule that grows up to a foot in length. Superstitions sprang up about the curious "horns," which were thought by some to be an ingredient in witches' potions. In Hampshire the plant was called Squatmore, for in Old English, *squat* was a bruise and *more* was a root. It was used to treat bruising, but the root, which resembles the carrot, was thought to cause madness if eaten. All parts of the plant are poisonous, so the belief was well-founded. Old English records from 1698 preserve the story of a man who baked a pie from the roots, thinking them to be those of *Eryngium maritimum*, the wild Sea Holly. While the roots of Sea Holly were reputed to act as an aphrodisiac, those of the Horned Poppy caused the man to become delirious. He became convinced his porcelain chamber pot was solid gold, and for reasons known only to him, broke it to bits.

The sap of the Horned Poppy is yellow, which led herbalists of the Middle Ages to attempt to treat jaundice with it. They believed that the "signature" of a plant—in this case, the colour of the sap—dictated how it could be employed medicinally, such as to treat the skin's yellow discoloration from jaundice. (They might as well have imagined the sap of Horned Poppy to cause the disease as well as cure it, for it does neither.)

Yellow-flowered *Glaucium flavum* (*flavum* means yellow) is a wildflower of Europe, northern Africa, and western Asia; it is naturalized in places in the British Isles and the American eastern seaboard. The form with orange-red flowers is often labelled as *G. corniculatum* (meaning horned), but is considered by many to be a variety or subspecies of *G. flavum*. Both forms feature deeply cut blue-grey leaves, and their branches' stems carry the bright flowers in late spring and summer. The display of dramatic seed pods overlaps with the blooming period, and culminates in a sculptural show of intertwined horns at season's end.

Seeds of the Horned Poppy may be sown in early spring where they are to grow, for the taproot makes transplanting a perilous operation. The plants may behave as biennials or persist as perennials in some locations. Full sun and sandy soil suit *Glaucium* best, though it performs admirably in any well-drained garden soil. In favourable spots the plants may seed themselves prolifically to establish handsome colonies. The Horned Poppy is an evocative addition to a seaside garden, where its blossoms, shed on the waves, tell of its wistful history.

The flowers of *Glaucium flavum*, ILLUSTRATION, are followed by dramatic seed pods, LEFT.

Helenium autumnale Compositae

SNEEZEWEED

Helenium autumnale, ABOVE and RIGHT, exhibits colour diversity throughout its range.

This plant suffers from two of the most misleading names. The colloquial Sneezeweed is totally unjustified—it categorically does not cause an allergic reaction. Colonists may have attempted to make a snuff from the leaves at one point, as Native Americans did for head colds, but he who sticks things up the nose deserves what he gets.

Equally inappropriate is the scientific name *Helenium*. It honours Helen of Troy, whose face launched a thousand ships (and for it, must have been the worse for wear). None of these ships ever made it to the New World, so Helen, or any other Greek, could not possibly have seen any of these lovely North American flowers. Legend holds that the flowers sprang from her tears, but for that to have happened, she would have needed to cry even more than the proverbial river. It has been speculated that the golden yellow flowers were likened to Helen's hair—she was reputed to be a blonde—but this is really stretching it. Too bad it doesn't honour a real heroine, such as Dolly Madison, whom I've always admired for personally saving the portrait of George Washington when the British sacked the White House during the War of 1812. Perhaps *Dollia* would be confused with *Dahlia*, however.

The only apt part of the name is the binomial *autumnale*, for the stately plants bloom late in the season. Indigenous to a vast area of North America, *Helenium autumnale* shows a diversity of colour and height in its range from Canada to Florida and Arizona. It is most numerous in New

England, however, where the plants, up to five feet tall, bloom in wet thickets and fields. The central knobbed disc of each flower has a collar of wedge-shaped rayflorets, each edged with three toothed notches. These silky petals are most often vivid yellow, but some are reddish brown or deep mahogany. Careful selection has produced pretty horticultural varieties in various rustic shades.

A tea brewed from the flowers was drunk in colonial days for fevers and the flu, and to expel worms, so perhaps we are fortunate it did not become Wormweed. *H. autumnale* first grew in English gardens in 1729, where it was warmly received. According to Graham Stuart Thomas, they are "easily grown in almost any soil short of a bog." The moisture-loving perennials benefit from division every few years, and the growth tips may be pinched out in early summer to promote bushy growth and a shorter stature. Sneezeweed is poisonous to cattle, and repugnant to insects.

The intensity of the flower colours necessitates that Sneezeweed not be mixed in a border with brilliant phlox, monarda, or mallows for fear of sparking a war the equivalent of the one caused by Helen herself. *H. autumnale* assorts best with ivorytinted flowers and bold foliage such as Plume Poppy, *Macleaya cordata*, Pigsqueak, *Bergenia cordifolia*, *Heuchera* 'Palace Purple', or Pearly Everlasting, *Anaphalis margaritacea*.

The genus *Heuchera* commemorates Johann Heinrich von Heucher, an eighteenth-century German botanist and professor of medicine. It is surprising how many American plants have German connections—botanists and gardeners in Germany, as well as England, France, Spain, and Linnaeus' own Sweden, were mad about the New World imports.

There are more than fifty species of the exclusively North American genus *Heuchera*, the most horticulturally important being *H. sanguinea*. Native to the Southwestern United States, it was discovered about 1846 by Dr. Adolph Wislizenus who became a Mexican War prisoner for his trouble. The specimen finally reached botanist George Engelmann in St. Louis, an expert on Mexican flora and a good friend of Asa Gray's. *H. sanguinea*, as he named it, was introduced to England in 1882. Shortly thereafter, Maria Theresa Earle wrote in her classic *Pot-pourri from a Surrey Garden* that she considered Coralbells to be "one of the most precious American flowers." Dr. Wislizenus would surely have concurred.

The deep green mounds of marbled, rounded leaves are topped by straight flowering stems, fifteen inches or taller. From these dangle tiny bell-shaped flowers of bright coral red; the specific epithet *sanguinea* means blood red. The flowers are produced over a long period, often from spring to autumn with good care in moist,

Heuchera americana
ALUM ROOT

Heuchera sanguinea
CORALBELLS

White Coralbells, ABOVE, contrast with their red counterparts. Foliage of *Salvia officinalis* 'Icterina' and variegated *Iris pallida* set off Coralbells and *Sedum spectabile*, RIGHT. ILLUSTRATION, *Heuchera americana*.

humus-enriched soil. Selections with various tints have been made over the years, as well as hybrids with *H. micrantha*, introduced to England in 1827 from the Pacific Northwest. The variety 'Alba' possesses the most enduring charms. It was the subject of a folk round that children used to sing and perhaps still do:

> White Coralbells
> Along a slender stalk
> Lilies of the valley
> Dress my garden walk.
>
> Oh, how I wish
> I could hear them ring
> That would only happen
> When the fairies sing.

The roots of Midwest native *H. americana* were so astringent that settlers called it Alum Root. This country flower is rarely cultivated, although it was introduced to England in 1656. Its panicles of pale green or pale purple bells, up to two feet tall, are borne over handsomely mottled foliage. The young leaves are flushed and veined with a coppery colour, and are deep red on the undersides. Gertrude Jekyll called it Satin-leaf, and said "the beauty of the plant is in the colour and texture of the foliage."

Coralbells and Alum Root are exemplary choices for the front of a traditional border, planted in masses to complement *Artemisia* 'Silver Mound', variegated sage, Partridge Feather, or Lamb's Ears. White Coralbells are exceedingly pretty with cranesbills and campanulas. Heucheras are also effective scattered in clumps along a meandering path.

Heuchera Saxifragaceae

I first encountered this startling plant when I took a shortcut down an alley near my house. A picket-fenced little jewel of a garden, hidden from the street, shone with phlox, cosmos, and roses. The tomatoes and squash competed for space in the classic cottage garden tradition. Lining the fence was a magnificent scarlet torch of a plant that was new to me. I asked the elderly gardeners the name of the plant; they called it Skyrocket and had grown it for many years.

The scientific name is *Ipomopsis rubra*, from the Greek *ipo*, to strike forcibly, and *opsis*, sight, while the species name *rubra* means red. A well-named plant, I must say—unless one is to believe the derivation is from *ips*, a worm—in which case the red flower with a striking appearance becomes one resembling a red worm. I'll take the former version.

I. rubra is a native of the southern United States. It is possible that Spanish explorers introduced the plant to Europe. Linnaeus named it *Polemonium rubrum*; it thereafter became a *Gilia*, and finally during this century, an *Ipomopsis*. A closely related species, *I. aggregata* of the Southwest, is shorter but similar. It is also called Skyrocket or Scarlet Gilia.

The finely-dissected leaves of *I. rubra* are held on ram-rod stiff stems rising from four to six feet in height. The country name Standing Cypress alludes to the needle-thin foliage and stature of the plant.

Ipomopsis aggregata
SKYROCKET

Ipomopsis rubra
STANDING CYPRESS

I. rubra dominates a cottage garden, LEFT. *I. aggregata* and *Zinnia grandiflora* share a mason jar, ABOVE.

The flowers, of course, are the main attraction, blooming in July and August. The five-petalled tubular blossoms are about an inch long, and bloom along the main stem and smaller auxiliary branches; they "are covered," wrote Peter Henderson, "nearly their whole length with brilliant scarlet flowers." They attract hummingbirds and flower lovers alike with their fiery colour.

Biennial flowers, such as Standing Cypress and Skyrocket, often suffer from a deep-seated prejudice. Some gardeners refuse to grow anything but perennials—permanent plants. Those that grow annuals often want instant gratification, or at least spectacular effects during the current season. They will be patient for the cosmos or dahlias to glorify the garden later in the season, but waiting an extra year for a biennial is out of the question. This is a pity, since I can hardly picture a garden where *I. rubra* or *I. aggregata* could not be used to spectacular advantage.

Sown in late spring in open sandy ground in a sunny situation, the plants form a ferny rosette the first year. The trick is to plant seeds in two successive years; the self-sown seedlings will thereafter bloom in alternate years. Although the seedlings are able to survive cold winters, they are unable to tolerate standing water about their roots. They can be planted on higher ground and protected with a light mulch, or grown in pots and stored in a cold frame for the winter. The flowering stem begins to grow the following spring, culminating in a floral extravaganza blazing in the summer heat.

Ipomopsis Polemoniaceae

Lathyrus latifolius Leguminosae

EVERLASTING PEA

Flowers of *Lathyrus latifolius*, ABOVE, and its look-alike, *L. grandiflorus*, LEFT, cloak a rustic fence.

There are trade-offs involved in growing Everlasting Pea, *Lathyrus latifolius*, as opposed to its Sweet Pea cousin, *Lathyrus odoratus*. The latter is a beloved annual, valued for its powerful fragrance. The former is a valued perennial, a pretty and lasting addition to the garden, hence the common name, but without a scent. It is sometimes called the Perennial "Sweet" Pea, but this is a misnomer, on the order of calling *The Far Horizons* a "classic" movie.

L. latifolius is a native of France, and has been grown in England at least since the sixteenth century. Gerard admired the "most beautifull flowers like those of Pease, the middle part whereof is a bright red, tending to red-Purple in graine; the outer leaves somewhat lighter inclining to a blush." Parkinson similarly liked the "purplish pease like blossomes . . . very beautifull to behold," but he surprisingly praises their "pretty sent or smell." Since Sweet Pea was not introduced to England until nearly fifty years after Parkinson's death, this remark could not have stemmed from a case of mistaken identity. We must assume that Parkinson had a very perceptive olfactory system.

Classified as a "garden escapee" in parts of Britain, *L. latifolius* is often known as Wild Pea. It is similarly naturalized in parts of North America, especially near abandoned farms. It is found in hedgerows and along railway embankments.

Everlasting Pea climbs by means of tendrils, as most peas do, to several feet in height. The stems are winged and hold pairs of veined leaves two to four inches long; *latifolius* refers to their breadth. The flowers feature the typical keel of the pea, surrounded by the banner petal. From five to fifteen in a cluster, they are held on wiry stems. Bright rose purple is the blossom colour most often seen, although variations such as pure white are found.

Victorian Shirley Hibberd especially admired this white form of Everlasting Pea, calling it "one of the finest in its class to train to the walls of an artificial ruin or about any quaint edifice that needs the embellishment of a delicate but riotous vegetation." I suppose they might look pretty growing on real ruins as well. Jane Loudon, who was an important trendsetter in Victorian England, recommended a bower of Everlasting Peas to cover an arbour. They have been used in this manner for generations, as well as for trellises and fences. They may be allowed to tumble across rockwork or screen unsightly objects such as stumps or statues of gnomes.

Modern gardeners find that Everlasting Pea, which thrives in part to full sun in almost any soil, may be trained into large evergreens. The long-lasting summer display of flowers is especially effective against the foliage of the gold-leaved junipers. Entire stems may be cut to spill artfully from large arrangements, or smaller clusters tucked into smaller bouquets.

Liatris is an unlikely looking member of the Daisy tribe. The petal-less flowers are born on stiff spikes and are about as representative of the classic daisy flowers as Donna Reed of the Native Americans. The flowers are highly unusual in the entire floral kingdom in that the flowers open from the top of the stalk down, rather than the other way around like delphiniums and veronicas. The genus *Liatris* is confined to North America, and most of the forty or so species are found east of the Rocky Mountains. They must be considered among the rascally genera, for the species hybridize readily in the wild. Their overlapping territories and propensity for crossing in nature makes positive identification difficult, even for the experts.

The most recognizable of the species include Button Snakeroot, *L. pycnostachya*, and Gayfeather, *L. spicata*. The common names are somewhat interchangeable, for in folk medicine, a poultice of the corms of many species of *Liatris* was applied in case of snakebite. A tea brewed from the roots was also a remedy for kidney problems, colic, and sore throats. The derivation of the scientific name is obscure, but it may be from *lyaeus*, an epithet for Dionysus, meaning loosener. The Greek god of wine and fertility—a happy combination—was

Liatris
Compositae

Liatris pycnostachya
BUTTON SNAKEROOT

Liatris spicata
GAYFEATHER

A section of the rock alpine garden at the Denver Botanic Gardens, LEFT, features wildflowers of the American plains and foothills, including *Liatris spicata*. ILLUSTRATION, top blossoms on the stalk of *L. pycnostachya* open first.

lyaeus in his ability to free men from care. No mention is made of his curing snakebite, although that certainly would relieve a victim from care.

L. pycnostachya is native to the Great Plains from South Dakota to Louisiana and Texas. It was introduced to England in 1732, but named by André Michaux in 1803 in his *Flora boreali-Americana*. It is notable for its height, up to five feet. The adjective *pycnostachya* means with dense spikes.

L. spicata was known to European botanists by 1636. It grows to two feet and forms clumps of a foot or more. *Spicata* refers to the spiked flower stalks, although this does not distinguish it in any way from the rest of its relatives. This species grows wild throughout a good portion of the country east of the Rockies. The feathery appearance of the flowering spikes, a grand sight in full bloom, led to the common name Gayfeather or Blazing Star.

Button Snakeroot and Gayfeather fare well in free-draining soil in a sunny position. They are extremely resistant to heat and drought. The lavender-purple spikes of flowers make longlasting additions to the garden from July onward into autumn. The flower spikes will last for weeks in water when cut for arrangements. *Liatris* may be propagated from seed, but the home gardener will find the easiest method of increase is by division. In the early spring, while the plants are still dormant, lift clumps and divide the corms with a knife or pruning shears.

Button **S**nakeroot brightens a courtyard, LEFT, and punctuates *Rudbeckia hirta*, *Mimulus cardinalis*, and *Echinacea purpurea*, RIGHT.

Lilium Liliaceae

Lilium canadense MEADOW LILY

Lilium philadelphicum WOOD LILY

Lilium superbum TURK'S-CAP LILY

Lilium tigrinum TIGER LILY

Gardeners have long had a love affair with the lily. The pristine white Madonna Lily, *L. candidum*, is one of the oldest cultivated flowers. The New World held lovely new lilies that would captivate the settlers and Europeans alike. Jane Colden described two species growing in New York.

The first, *L. canadense*, must have reminded her of the pendant *L. martagon* of Europe, for she called it "Lilium Murtagon, Yellow Lily the flowers hanging downwards." The Meadow Lily, as it is often called, is a graceful one, found in moist meadows from Quebec to Alabama, as far west as Indiana. Miss Colden noted that the specimen she described "was taken from one that grows wild in a swamp," blooming in July. The flower colour is variable, from pale yellow to red, and the petals are peppered with tiny paprika-coloured spots. Each bell-shaped flower dangles elegantly from a long stalk emanating from the top of a straight stem. The stems grow from two to five feet with whorls of leaves three to six inches long. The Meadow Lily may have been grown in England as early as 1535, and was certainly known there by 1620.

Miss Colden also encountered Wood Lily, *L. philadelphicum*, "with the flowers standing upright." It is the only species in the eastern half of the continent with up-facing flowers. Wood Lily favours dry, sandy soils in light shade from New England to the Rocky Mountains. The stems are from one to three feet high, topped by solitary or clustered cup-shaped flowers. The petals are orange-red, liberally sprinkled with chocolate spots. Wood Lily "Grows upon Upland & flowers in June," according to the pioneer New York botanist. Despite its wide range, this lily is not really plentiful, and is difficult to accommodate in civilized gardens. John Bartram sent bulbs to the Chelsea Physic Garden in 1737.

One of the real showstoppers of American lilies—or the entire genus, for that matter, is *L. superbum*. Its name means, quite literally, superb (and it should be pronounced in a like manner, not as "super bum," which I have heard on occasion). Robust and stately, this lily grows from four to eight feet in height, and blooms with up to forty flowers in July. The petals recurve from the down-facing flowers, hence the folk name Turk's-cap. The flowers are glowing orange-red, bright green in the interior, with mahogany-purple spots. Like the other two species, the leaves are held in whorls. *L. michauxii*, found by André Michaux, is a closely related and similar plant of the Southeast.

L. superbum grows wild in many eastern states in wet fields, although there is no record that Miss Colden ever saw it. It first bloomed in the English garden of Peter Collinson in 1738, sent by his friend Bartram. The flowers had such an impact on Collinson that he decided then and there to concentrate on American plants, on which he became a leading authority.

North American lilies can be successfully grown in environments that duplicate, as closely as possible, their native habitats. Moist, organically enriched soil, slightly acidic, is to the liking of *L. canadense* and *L. superbum*, while *L. philadelphicum* must be kept drier. They may be grown from seed, but since the seedlings take several years to bloom, it is best to purchase small, flowering-size bulbs.

Another species of lily from the other side of the globe was to eclipse all the others for a time, and find a lasting home in the cottage garden. Tiger Lily, *L. tigrinum*, had been grown by the Japanese, Koreans, and Chinese for a thousand years before it was introduced to Western horticulture from Canton in 1804 by William Kerr, a collector from Kew Gardens. The Orientals cultivated Tiger Lily for its edible bulb. I know gardeners who would sooner turn cannibal than eat a lily. Clumps of Tiger Lily may persist for generations, outlasting the buildings they were planted to surround, thereby achieving a wild status.

The flowers of Tiger Lily bloom vibrant orange on four to five foot stems in midsummer. The spotted petals of the pendant flowers also recurve in Turk's-cap fashion. It is odd that the lily was likened to a striped tiger, not a spotted panther. It is difficult, however, to imagine the Indian princess in *Peter Pan* with the name Leopard Lily.

L. superbum is among the most graceful lilies, LEFT and BELOW. ILLUSTRATION, *L. philadelphicum*.

A PORTFOLIO OF ANTIQUE SPECIES

The family Lobeliaceae, which some botanists regard as part of the larger bluebell tribe, Campanulaceae, is an incredibly diverse one. It includes the trailing annual valued since before Victorian times for summer display, as well as thirty-foot-tall tree lobelias from the Mountains of the Moon in eastern Africa. North America has its representatives as well, including two hardy herbaceous perennials, *Lobelia cardinalis* and *L. siphilitica*.

The genus is named for Flemish botanist Matthias de l'Obel (1538–1616) who served as botanist to James I, and helped to straighten out the mismatched illustrations in the first edition of Gerard's *Herball*. It is interesting to note that l'Obel's family took its name originally from the white poplar or "Abele" tree; the flowers in this genus commemorate a man who was named for a tree.

L. cardinalis is found in the wild from New Brunswick to Florida and as far west as Texas. It thrives in moist meadows and along stream banks. Victorian writer and gardener Jane Loudon told how the plant was first sent from the French colony of Canada to the royal gardens in Paris, from which Parkinson obtained it in 1627. When Henrietta Maria, queen to Charles I, first saw the startlingly brilliant flowers, she reportedly "laughed excessively, and said that the colour reminded her of the scarlet stockings of a Cardinal." Cardinal Flower created a stir throughout England, if not as mirthful. It was imported ten years later from America by the younger Tradescant, who generally receives credit for its introduction.

The intensely red flowers, blooming on two to four foot spikes in late summer, have long fascinated even gardeners with a penchant for pastels. The flowers measure up to an inch and a half long, and the lower lip is cleft into three thin lobes, while the upper lip is two-lobed. The plants grow successfully in organically rich, moist soil, and are best left to their own devices in waterside plantings with some shade. Overly aggressive neighbours are detrimental.

Great Lobelia, *L. siphilitica*, received its

Lobelia cardinalis, LEFT, enlivens a shady bank with vivid colour. Its blue cousin, *L. siphilitica*, ABOVE, is more subtle.

Lobelia cardinalis
CARDINAL FLOWER

Lobelia siphilitica
GREAT LOBELIA

unsavoury Latin name from Linnaeus himself, who had been told that a remedy for venereal disease was decocted by Native Americans from the plant. This Indian treatment excited great anticipation among European doctors. The Superintendent of Indian Affairs, Sir William Johnson, purchased the secret of preparing the treatment from the natives, but it was to prove useless. The Indians got mere trinkets for Manhattan; there is a small satisfaction in knowing they came out ahead in at least one deal. Nevertheless, gardeners are stuck with the name.

Great Lobelia inhabits roughly the same territory as Cardinal Flower, and is similar in its cultural requirements. The flowers of *L. siphilitica* are just slightly smaller than those of its scarlet cousin, but are characterized by a pouting lower lip with white stripes and a coloration of true blue. The flowers are held on erect stalks growing to two or three feet.

Although the secret for curing venereal disease has been lost (if it ever existed—syphilis did not exist in America until introduced by Europeans) both lobelias had other medicinal uses by Native Americans and early colonists. It was an ingredient, oddly enough, in love potions. Tea made from the roots or leaves was drunk for colds, nosebleeds, headaches, and stomach troubles. The leaves of a related species, *L. inflata*, were smoked by Native Americans to relieve asthma, bronchitis, and coughs. The plant was traditionally used as an emetic, and one less-than-charming folk name is Pukeweed.

Lobelia Lobeliaceae

Mentzelia
Loasaceae

Mentzelia laevicaulis
BLAZING STAR

Mentzelia lindleyi
CALIFORNIA STAR

ILLUSTRATION, *M. lindleyi*. Blazing Star shines at dawn, BELOW, and in an arrangement, RIGHT.

Blazing Star is an unusual flower from a relatively obscure family consisting of annuals, biennials, and perennials of the American Southwest, Mexico, and the West Indies. Sixteenth-century German botanist Christian Mentzel is commemorated by the genus name. *Mentzelia* belongs to the Loasaceae, an equally obscure tribe principally noted for bristle-haired plants, sometimes with stinging qualities, that are colloquially called Chili Nettles.

As it stands, few gardeners—even in the western United States, where *M. laevicaulis* grows wild—have ever seen it, except perhaps from a speeding car. This is all the more remarkable in that more than a century ago, Peter Henderson was well-acquainted with the genus and recommended that the "white, showy flowers . . . common on the western plains . . . are all easily raised from seed."

M. laevicaulis was first described by Torrey and Gray from specimens collected in Wyoming. The satin-textured flowers are among the loveliest of the Old West. Even the name Blazing Star has a certain cowboy culture ring to it. The pale yellow flowers open at dusk, revealing a bundle of feathery stamens surrounded by the luminous petals—this is the blazing part of the star. Each blossom measures up to four inches in diameter and closes the following morning, although the flowers will stay open on cloudy days. The biennial plants grow as tall as four feet, and the cleft sage-green leaves are held on silvery stems.

The stems and leaves of most mentzelias are clad with fine hairs, except for *M. laevicaulis*, which has stems smooth at the base. *Laevis* means smooth, and *caulis* means stem. The family is often called Stickleaf for its fine Velcro-like barbed hairs. In Texas it is known as *buena mujer*, good woman, for this clinging, unshakeable quality. (It has not, to my knowledge, been called Get-off-my-back-weed.) The oil-rich seeds of Blazing Star were pounded by Native Americans to make a cake.

Blazing Star blooms from June to September on sun-drenched plains from Montana to New Mexico, and westward into Utah, California, and Washington. It favours sandy or gravelly soils and thrives on heat and low rainfall. The flowers are best sown where they are to grow, for the very taproot that insures their survival during periods of drought makes transplanting them very tricky. Gardeners in less arid regions may be successful in growing them on slopes with sharply draining soil.

Annual *M. lindleyi* from California, named for English botanist John Lindley, was formerly known as *Bartonia aurea*, named for American botanist Dr. Benjamin Barton. Confusion about the name has reigned since it was introduced in 1834.

California Star grows from one to nearly three feet, and the hairy, toothed leaves and succulent stems are characteristic of the Stick leaf family. It is tolerant of more moisture than *M. laevicaulis*, though it, too, will perform best during a hot, dry summer. These plants are also best seeded *in situ* and thinned to six inches apart. The five-petalled golden flowers shade to orange at the base of the petals, which highlights the prominent fluff of stamens. Henderson proclaimed it "a splendid annual," so we must assume the western wildflower grew well in his Jersey City garden. He described how the blossoms "have quite a metallic luster when the sun shines upon them," although this would only be apparent in the morning. California Stars open at sundown, releasing a sweet fragrance, highly attractive to gardeners, but intended as nocturnal pollinators.

Monarda Labiatae

Monarda citriodora LEMON MINT

Monarda didyma BEE BALM

Monarda punctata HORSEMINT

The name of this genus of the mint family Labiatae commemorates Dr. Nicholas Monardes, a Spanish physician and naturalist who published the first book on the flora of America. This volume was translated into English in 1577 as *Joyfull newes out of the new founde worlde*, not the sort of title botanists are prone to using these days, but indicative of the frenzied excitement about the floral wonders being introduced to Europe.

The friendship and shared passion for plants between John Bartram and Peter Collinson was responsible for the introduction of a number of favourite American perennials. Bartram sent the seed of *Monardo didyma* to his English friend in 1744. He had collected them in Oswego, on the shore of Lake Ontario, where they were used to make a pleasant minty tea. This Oswego Tea was an immediate hit, and by 1760 the leaves were being sold in the Covent Garden Market.

The fragrance of these aromatic leaves was likened to that of the Bergamot orange, a hybrid between a lemon and an orange. It was originally raised in the Italian town of Bergamo, and oil from the fragrant fruit was used in perfumery as early as 1688. The American plant subsequently became known in some quarters as Sweet Bergamot. Gardening clergyman William Hanbury recommended that *M. didyma* "ought to be propagated plentifully in the kitchen garden for the sake of the leaves to afford tea, which is highly agreeable, refreshing and said to be very wholesome."

M. didyma proved much too pretty to be kept solely in the confines of the kitchen garden. The tubular flowers of Oswego Tea form a shaggy red crown atop three- to four-foot stems with serrated, paired leaves. Bees find the flowers irresistible and the plant is often called Bee Balm. The flowers are somewhat variable in the wild, from blood red to rosy violet, and a number of horticultural selections have been made over the years, from pink and mahogany red to pure white.

Oswego Tea grows wild from New England to Georgia, and westward to Tennessee and Minnesota. Jane Colden called it Red Mint, and said it was grown in gardens as well as "wild in the Mohawks Country." The tea must have been among the most pleasant Indian and settler treatments for any number of ills, including colic, measles, insomnia, and fevers. The flowers attract notice in midsummer in thickets and along stream banks in moist woodlands, not to mention in gardens in town and country alike.

Horsemint, *M. punctata* and Lemon Mint, *M. citriodora*, have never received the acclaim in ornamental gardening as has Oswego Tea, but they are highly attractive and aromatic as well. Horsemint is a native flower in drier soils from Vermont to the Great Lakes, and throughout the south from Florida to Arkansas. As might be expected with such a wide geographic distribution, this annual or short-lived perennial displays varying characteristics. The charming flowers are often pale yellow with degrees of purple or pink spots; *punctata* means spotted. They are held in whorls along stems growing as tall as four feet. Annual or biennial Lemon Mint grows from Missouri and Nebraska to Arizona. The flowers are held in tiers on stems up to two feet high. Purple or green bracts encase the pink or yellow flowers stippled with purple spots.

An oil extracted from the leaves of Horsemint is high in thymol, used as an antiseptic and to expel worms. The oil, now manufactured synthetically, was formerly derived from species of thyme grown in Europe. During the First World War, when the thyme fields were destroyed, *M. punctata* was grown commercially in the United States to supply thymol to hospitals.

It should come as no surprise that the oil has traditionally been employed for equine rubdowns. Gardeners, myself included, have been known to concoct a homemade liniment for their own tired muscles. It is extremely refreshing, and imparts that gentrified fresh-from-the-stable fragrance.

Bee Balm and penstemons complement a glazed pot, PREVIOUS PAGE, LEFT. A brew from the leaves and flowers of *Monarda didyma*, PREVIOUS PAGE, RIGHT, called Oswego Tea, was preferred by rebellious American patriots who boycotted British tea; a selected purplish form deviates from the standard red coloration of the species. A whorl of the spotted flowers of *Monarda punctata* is shown, ILLUSTRATION. Lemon Mint, *M. citriodora*, RIGHT, is highly aromatic and ornamental.

Oenothera Onagraceae

The name for the genus *Oenothera* is derived from an old Greek one for an unknown plant, but the ancient Greeks never knew these endemic New World flowers. *O. biennis*, native to the eastern United States, has long been grown in gardens, and now claims parts of Europe as its natural domain as well. The seeds were sent from Virginia to Italy in 1619, and to England shortly thereafter. It was heralded as the Prime-rose Tree of Virginia. The common name Evening Primrose is rather misleading, not only because oenotheras are not related to diminutive, spring-blooming primulas, but this is a rocket of a plant, which grows up to five feet high and blooms in summer. The flower opens at dusk with a visible movement; the poet John Keats recalled how he was "startled by the leap of buds into ripe flowers."

Because the flower opens at night, it became a symbol of humility and reward. We have Victorian poetess Rebecca Hey to thank for this association in her 1833 volume of poems *The Moral of Flowers*. Explaining its lone nightly vigil, the flower speaks:

> *Eve is my noon—at this still hour,*
> *When softly sleeps each sister flower,*
> *Sole watcher of the dusky bower*
> *I joy to be,*
> *And conscious feel the pale moon shower*
> *Her light on me.*

The Evening Primrose goes on to advise humans to shun "tumult and glare and vanity" as it has. The rest of the family is altogether more boisterous. The flowers of aptly-named Sundrop, *O. fruticosa*, shine against the deep olive-green foliage that is often tinged with red. The clear yellow blooms are one to two inches wide and bloom heavily in midsummer. The perennial plants are variable in the wild, found from Massachusetts to Florida, and east to Alabama. Sundrop favours a moisture-retentive soil in sun or part shade, where it must be given full rein to colonize, for it can become aggressive to a fault. Gardeners take exception to its Latin binomial *fruticosa*, meaning shrubby—which it is not, and with the sometimes common name Swedish Buttercup—which likewise is not applicable.

Thomas Nuttall is credited with the discovery of perennial or biennial Matted Evening Primrose, *O. caespitosa*. I am not nearly as fond of the colloquial name—suggesting a shaggy dog—as I am of the flower. To my mind, it is a riveting beauty of an altogether handsome genus. A low-growing mound of serrated, downy leaves enhances the three-inch wide ethereal flowers, which open pure white and take on subtle tints of pink and lavender as they age. Sunrise is the best time for viewing, as the early sun illuminates the blossoms. *Caespitosa* means tufted, and it is suggested that it should be pronounced kie-spi-toe-sa. The flower is native to Nebraska and South Dakota, and neighbouring states both southward and westward.

O. speciosa also bears a muddled common name, White Evening Primrose. It is not, of course, a primrose, nor does it bloom at night, and it is extensively distributed in the wild from Missouri to Texas, and finally into Mexico. The Latin binomial *speciosa*, meaning showy, needs no disclaimer. The upfacing blossoms, measuring two to three inches across, are a pale shade of pink, with a delicate tracery of white veins. *O. speciosa* can be perennial, biennial, or even annual, depending on growing conditions. Like *O. caespitosa*, the plants are best situated in well-drained sandy soil where water will not collect around the crown of the plant. Self-sown seedlings will often find a better location for themselves than that originally selected by the gardener.

Oenothera biennis EVENING PRIMROSE

Oenothera caespitosa
MATTED EVENING PRIMROSE

Oenothera fruticosa SUNDROP

Oenothera speciosa
WHITE EVENING PRIMROSE

O. biennis, OPPOSITE, blooms with *Centaurea cyanus*. Other species include, RIGHT, TOP TO BOTTOM: *O. caespitosa*, *O. speciosa*, and *O. fruticosa*.

The native poppy of European cornfields, *Papaver rhoeas*, has long been an advertisement for poor farming. The seeds are practically indestructible, having been known to germinate after being buried for forty years. Modern herbicides have pretty much dispatched the pest, to the disappointment of painters and poets, but much to the relief of farmers. In days past they called it Redweed, Canker, or simply Headache. It was not always so despised. In ancient times, the poppy was the symbol of the earth goddess Cybele, and it was believed that poppies were essential to the health of the crop. This may have been a comforting excuse not to tackle the impossible task of weeding them.

The French are kinder, calling them by the folk name *Coquelicot*, a diminutive of rooster, and it is said that the poppy bends its head when the cock crows. Hills and fields in Europe and Asia are resplendent in summer with the bright annual wildflowers, and they are now naturalized in parts of North America.

Scorn for poppies was replaced by affection when, after the battle at Flanders Field during the First World War, the battle-scarred earth bloomed scarlet with their flowers. Long-dormant seeds had risen to the surface of the disturbed soil after the burials, and the flowers came to represent the blood shed by the soldiers. A red poppy—a Flanders Poppy—came to be worn on Remembrance Day. John McRae's poem was first published in *Punch* in 1915. Its most famous lines read:

> *In Flanders fields they blow*
> *Between the crosses, row on row.*

The pastel Shirley Poppies were selected from a single white-edged flower of *P. rhoeas*, discovered by the Rev. William Wilks. They are named not for the vicar's wife, but for his English village. He commenced his twenty-year labour of love about 1880, crossing and re-crossing to produce larger

Robert Burns wrote:

> *But pleasures are like poppies spread,*
> *You seize the flow'r, its bloom is shed;*
> *Or like the snow falls in the river,*
> *A moment white—then melts forever;*

P. nudicaule, ABOVE, glows in the sun.
P. rhoeas carpets a field, OPPOSITE
ABOVE AND BELOW.

blossoms in varying shades and patterns. The flowers lack the black patch at the base of the petals that the wild species has.

Seeds of Iceland Poppy, *P. nudicaule*, arrived in England in 1730 from Siberia, not from Iceland as may be supposed. A closely related species, *P. radicatum*, is one of four plants that survive on the frigid northern coast of Greenland, so the misnomer is not really an important one. Besides, Iceland Poppy has a better ring to it than Siberian Poppy. *P. nudicaule* manages to thrive in latitudes approaching the arctic circle. *Nudicaule* means bare-stemmed, further conjuring an image of shivering plants. The amazing part has been its adaptability to warmer climes. The best success with the brilliantly coloured annual is still achieved, however, by gardeners in cool regions such as the mountains or in maritime zones. There Iceland Poppies will bloom with abandon in stained glass tones of red, orange, yellow, and white, all the more brilliant when the sun shines.

The crinkled petals have long been a source of fascination. In *Proserpina*, Victorian writer and social reformer John Ruskin observed that "When the flower opens, it seems a deliverance from torture; the two imprisoning green leaves fall to the ground, and the aggrieved corolla smoothes itself in the sun, and comforts itself as it can, but remains visibly crushed and hurt to the end of its days." It must have taken a Herculean effort on Ruskin's part to concoct such a black story from one of nature's gayest flowers. Fleeting though they may be, poppies are pleasures.

Papaver Papaveraceae

Papaver nudicaule ICELAND POPPY

Papaver rhoeas FLANDERS POPPY

The penstemons are the pride of the American West. The flowers are so charming, the colours so vivid, and the species so varied, that many gardeners find that specializing in them is a rewarding experience.

Penstemon is derived from the Greek words *pente*, five, and *stemon*, a stamen, an obvious allusion to the stamens of the flower. It is sometimes incorrectly spelled with an extra "t" as *Pentstemon*. The flowers are commonly called Beard Tongues from a sterile stamen in the throat of the flower that often bears a tuft of hairs. The image of a hairy tongue is difficult for me to picture, and this unappetizing allusion, I think, tends to discourage the squeamish from cultivating them.

The enormous genus *Penstemon*, some 250 species strong, is endemic to North America, with the exception of one straggler in northeastern Asia. It is of the Scrophulariaceae, so it should come as no surprise that they often bear a resemblance to related snapdragons, foxgloves, and mullein. Less likely relatives include *Castilleja*, *Mimulus*, and a Chinese tree, the splendid *Paulownia tomentosa*.

The two- to four-foot flowering stems of Scarlet Bugler, *P. barbatus*, paint the foothills of Colorado and Utah red during the summer. Introduced to England in 1784 under the name *Chelone barbata*, this penstemon is one of the most adaptable of the genus and can be grown successfully in most parts of America as well as the British Isles. The lower lip of the tubular blossom curls back, while the upper lip projects forward jauntily. I once saw a picture of Joan Crawford wearing a terribly fashionable hat that unintentionally mimicked the flower's design. These scarlet bugles are touched with pink in their throats.

Rocky Mountain Penstemon, *P. strictus*, is a cool-coloured counterpart to Scarlet Bugler. An introduction from the western states, it arrived in England during the early nineteenth century, just when carpet bedding schemes of tightly pinched annuals were taking the horticultural world by storm. The newcomer, despite its jewel-toned blossoms of violet-blue, was decidedly too wild for the Victorians. The glaucous leaves set off the display of flowers on spikes growing from two to four feet in June.

P. pinifolius was first described in Coulter's Botanical Gazette in 1881 by Alfred

P. barbatus sparks an arrangement with white *Echinacea purpurea*, *Macleaya cordata*, cactus, and pods, RIGHT. *P. pinifolius*, ABOVE, blazes with blossoms.

Greene, the pre-eminent botanist on the west coast. Greene is a fascinating character in western botany, carrying on a raging feud with Asa Gray at Harvard, albeit from a safe distance at the University of California at Berkeley. Fundamental differences separated the two men, not the least being Greene's dismissal of Charles Darwin's newfangled evolutionary theories in *Origin of Species* (1859), which Gray had embraced. Hasty about publishing accounts of new species without Gray's advice, Greene often failed to take into account climatic differences that might produce slight deviations in appearance within a singular species. Gray wrote, "It does not require any knowledge of botany and only a little of the rules to name a plant . . . ," something at which Greene excelled. He charged Gray with prejudice toward him, saying that the elder botanist had relegated him to "the limbo of conceited cranks," which, ironically, is a fair assessment of his place in botanic history. Indeed, few of the three thousand or so of Greene's "new" species have been accepted by botanists. This penstemon is one of the exceptions.

Pinifolius alludes to the leaves that resemble pine needles, but the plant's main attraction is its prolific production of bright orange flowers. Its low mounds of foliage grow to ten inches or so, and the blaze of flowers in summer's heat earned it the folk designation Prairie Fire. Like most of the penstemons, it thrives in a sunny position in sandy, free-draining soil. The bright, tubular flowers of Prairie Fire attract hummingbirds down to ground level for its nectar. Those who keep cats may wish to consider if their nerves can stand the drama this combination provokes.

Penstemon Scrophulariaceae

Penstemon barbatus SCARLET BUGLER

Penstemon pinifolius PRAIRIE FIRE

Penstemon strictus
ROCKY MOUNTAIN PENSTEMON

Physostegia Labiatae

Both perennial species of *Physostegia* discussed here inhabit swampy thickets and wet prairies from the eastern seaboard as far west as Kansas and Oklahoma. The flowers resemble those of a very fastidious snapdragon, held in tight, orderly bundles atop rigid stems growing from two to five feet high. The botanic differences between *P. virginiana* and *P. formosior* are inconsequential to the gardener, but the flowers of the latter are usually a paler shade and its structure is somewhat looser.

The lilac-pink flowers of *P. virginiana* have occupied a valued position in the autumn border since its English introduction in 1683. The plants form colonies with deep green, toothed leaves. Too much water encourages the running rootstock to fairly sprint about the garden. Less kindness will curb this tendency. Selection has produced varieties with rosier flowers bordering on magenta; a white form blooms earlier, in August, and is a model of decorum when it comes to spreading.

P. formosior is as trouble free as its cousin, and the flowers are held in less dense clusters over longer, thinner leaves. It imparts an airier feeling to a planting. Both species merit inclusion in sunny or partially shaded gardens for their longlast-

Clumps of the white form of *Physostegia virginiana* enhance silver shafts of *Artemisia ludoviciana*, as well as brilliant *Rudbeckia hirta* and *Phlox paniculata*, LEFT.

Physostegia formosior
FALSE
DRAGON HEAD

Physostegia virginiana
OBEDIENCE

ing display in September and October. They make fine contrasting companions to Japanese Windflowers, whose colours they echo.

The stems of seed pods may be left on the plants in the winter to poke through the snow. The Latin name refers to the inflated calyx covering the seeds; *physa* is a bladder, and *stege* is a covering. Gardeners often have a time trying to wrap their tongues around the word *Physostegia*. The common name, which is only occasionally used, False Dragon Head is rather absurd, and stems from the fact the plants were once placed in the genus *Dracocephalum*, which is called Dragon Head. At the time of the transfer to a new genus—more than a hundred years ago—the designation as "false" may have held some validity; I wonder how many contemporary gardeners picture a masquerade party for dragons only, each wearing a mask—perhaps of St. George, St. Margaret, or Prince Charming.

The most delightful name, and the most appropriate, is Obedience. Hinges attaching the flowers to the stem allow them to be bent to one side or the other, as well as up and down. Remarkably, they will stay in this position to the delight of children. I have always felt a bit silly arranging the flowers before they are cut for bouquets, but I admit it is a pleasure.

Spikes of *P. formosior*, ABOVE, display a loose, airy structure. **T**he flowers of *P. virginiana*, LEFT, bring springtime gaiety to the autumn garden.

As the daisy flowers of America were discovered, many of them were conveniently placed by botanists into the genus *Rudbeckia*. Further investigation segregated the purple coneflowers as *Echinacea*, and a distinct group of western daisies as *Ratibida*. The origin of the scientific name is obscure. *Ratis* is a float or pontoon; *bidens* means with two teeth or prongs. I picture elderly sharks circling a yellow life raft, perhaps not what was intended. *R. columnifera* has more synonyms than a criminal on a most-wanted list.

Thomas Nuttall and fellow English collector John Bradbury share the credit for the discovery and introduction of *R. columnifera*. Bradbury first sent seed of Mexican Hat to the Liverpool Botanic Garden in 1810. Many of his western discoveries were published by an unscrupulous botanist, Frederick Pursh, who published Bradbury's descriptions of thirty-nine new species as his own. Bradbury felt justifiably defrauded, an opinion shared by Nuttall and, eventually, the botanic community.

The flowers of *R. columnifera* are distinguished by an enlarged cylindric disc, up to two inches high, surrounded by a skirt of ray-florets or petals that hang down. The petals, about an inch long, may be yel-

Ratibida columnifera
Compositae

MEXICAN HAT

Mexican Hat meets gracious living, LEFT. An elongated disc skirted with petals distinguishes *R. columnifera*, RIGHT.

low or rust, or bicoloured. The festive flowers invite a fanciful comparison to a Mexican Hat. Wiry, grey-green flower stems rise above the foliage from one to three feet in height. The pinnate leaves are dull green. Mexican Hat behaves as a short-lived perennial or biennial.

R. columnifera blooms from June to September on prairies from Montana to Colorado, north to Canada and south to Mexico. It grows easily in ordinary or even poor garden soil in a sunny site, and is easily grown from seed in either a greenhouse or in open ground. Started early under glass, Mexican Hat seedlings develop quickly for a showy first season. The flowers are effectively used in informal plantings where a meadow look is desired. They also merit inclusion in the most studiously composed perennial groupings. Here the reddish Mexican Hats take on an elegance planted with vibrant orange crocosmias, dahlias, and daylilies, with a backdrop of the dusky purple *Prunus cerasifera*.

 Linnaeus named the genus of American daisies in tribute to the two botanists Rudbeck, whom he succeeded at the university in Uppsala. The elder Rudbeck—both were named Olaf—undertook a project to catalogue all the plants that had so far been discovered in the world. He had completed two volumes of the massive work, illustrated with woodcuts, when a fire at the university in 1702 destroyed all but three copies of the book, as well as 10,000 illustrations for the completion of the work. The shock no doubt contributed to his death later the same year.

Peter Henderson was amazed and amused by the rapid spread of rudbeckias throughout the nation. "This genus acquired an enviable reputation in Europe as an ornamental flowering plant," he wrote in 1890, "and the seed was distributed by the Department of Agriculture at Washington, through the members of Congress, to several of the States that had passed stringent laws against the dissemination of 'weeds.'" So we have the U.S. federal government to thank for the summertime display in many parts of America.

Black-eyed Susan, *Rudbeckia hirta*, was originally confined to the prairie states, but began its social climb with its English introduction in 1714. Native Americans had

Rudbeckia Compositae

Rudbeckia hirta
BLACK-EYED SUSAN

Rudbeckia laciniata
GREEN-HEADED CONEFLOWER

Rudbeckia triloba
BROWN-EYED SUSAN

Two brassy American daisies—brown-eyed *Rudbeckia triloba*, fronted by *Helenium autumnale*—gleam in late summer at the Garden in the Woods near Boston, LEFT.

A PORTFOLIO OF ANTIQUE SPECIES

made a wash for sores and swelling from the leaves, and a root juice for earaches. English gardeners admired the three-foot plant for its five-inch wide, brassy golden-yellow flowers held above deep olive-green hairy (*hirta*) leaves and stems. The petals surround a central disc of deep brown that gives the flower its common name, although the identity of the beautiful Susan it commemorates will forever remain a mystery. Hybridists exploited the natural variability of the species to create the garden race of gaily-painted Gloriosa Daisies.

R. triloba is often called Brown-eyed Susan for convenience sake, although the binomial *triloba*, meaning three-lobed leaves, is a more accurate differentiation. Jane Colden made a notation in her botanic manuscript that "the Leaves are all harsh to the touch and the lower ones most so." Though both species have brown central discs and yellow ray-florets, the blossoms of *R. triloba* are smaller, about two inches across. They are produced in great profusion on much-branched stems growing to four feet. Brown-eyed Susan blooms in meadows in summer and early autumn from the Atlantic seaboard to Minnesota, and south to Georgia.

Parkinson detailed the journey of *R. laciniata* from a French settlement in Canada to the king's herbalist in Paris, and finally to the elder John Tradescant, who shared the new American daisy with Parkinson. It was originally classified in pre-Linnaean times as *Aconitum Helianthemum Canadense*, which would make it the Canadian Sunflower-Wolfsbane, a very odd combination indeed.

Green-headed Coneflower, as *R. laciniata* came to be called, is a vigorous perennial growing to six feet or more. Its green-coned flowers are ringed with drooping canary yellow petals in summer. The old-fashioned double form is called Golden Glow. The species is scientifically named for its foliage as well; *laciniata* refers to its deeply-cut leaves. Green-headed Coneflower is widely distributed in North America from southeastern Canada to Florida, westward beyond the Rocky Mountains. It was used in Native American medicine as a poultice for burns, and the young greens were cooked as an all-purpose spring tonic.

Hanbury recommended that the rudbeckias "be set in the borders of woods to which walks lead, as they delight in shade, and will be very ornamental to such places, though seen at a distance." Apparently the American daisies were a bit bright and bold for some tastes.

R. triloba, LEFT, and *R. laciniata*, BELOW, bloom.

R. hirta, RIGHT and OPPOSITE, flowers with abandon.

Saponaria officinalis is native to continental Europe and western Asia, and is a member of the carnation family, if not as highly esteemed. It was grown in England during the Middle Ages, when it was called Soapwort, Latherwort, or Crowsoap. Real soap was a costly and expensive luxury of the day, and as Gerard describes, the leaves of the plant were welcome to "yeelde out of themselves a certain juyce when they are bruised, which scoureth almost as well as sope." The name *Saponaria* is derived from the Latin *sapo*, meaning soap. Parkinson concurs that "wild sopewort is used in many places, to scour the country-women's treen [wooden bowls] and pewter vessels." It is interesting to note that Soapwort was already a wildflower in Britain during Parkinson's day, escaping from plantings near wool mills.

S. officinalis is a tenacious flower. Gerard astutely reported that "if they have but once taken good and sure rooting in any ground, it is impossible to destroy them." The double-flowered variety, 'Flore Pleno', which more closely displays the plant's kinship to the carnation family, was introduced from the Continent about 1630. The pale pink or white flowers, about an inch across, were grown in pots for indoor decoration as well as their delicate scent. This also helped to curb its spreading nature. It quickly superseded the single form in gardens, but the plant was already firmly entrenched in the wild, where country folk knew it as Bouncing Bet or Bouncing Bess. This name may have sprung from the image of the bloomered backside of a washerwoman, bobbing over her tub.

We know that colonists brought Bouncing Bet to America, although whether it was by design or accident remains a mystery. It most likely made a handy soap substitute, as well as a hair shampoo, and was certainly less harsh than lye soap. The leaves could be applied as a poultice for cuts, abrasions, and for treating the rash caused by Poison Ivy. A tea brewed from the leaves was a popular treatment for liver ailments, gout, and rheumatism.

Bouncing Bet took a liking to the new land and headed for the hills. "How gladly has she been welcomed to our fields and roadsides," wrote Alice Morse Earle. She marvelled at the plant's ability "in beautifying arid dust heaps and barren railroad cuts, with her tender opalescent pink tints. How wholesome and hearty her growth, how pleasant her fragrance. We can never see her too often, nor ever stigmatize her, as have been so many of our garden escapes, as 'Now a dreaded weed.'"

S. officinalis is quite the best of alley plants, where it blooms with hollyhocks and creeping bellflowers, oblivious to the rust and refuse. Bouncing Bet should not be despised for its social standing, however, and 'Flore Pleno' is a charming addition to beds and borders, especially in difficult spots where little else will prosper. The sweet blossoms are excellent for cutting. Gertrude Jekyll created an artful vignette with the double form of *S. officinalis*, pink penstemons, steely blue Globe Thistle, and sulphur yellow Hollyhock.

The double form of *Saponaria officinalis*, 'Flore Pleno', combines with alliums and Queen Anne's Lace, LEFT. Bouncing Bet colonizes a country road, ABOVE.

Saponaria officinalis
Caryophyllaceae

SOAPWORT

CHECKERBLOOM

The genus *Sidalcea* is comprised of species from western North America, the most important horticulturally being *S. malviflora*. The name accurately suggests that its blossoms resemble those of mallows.

The scientific name was formed from two related genera, *Sida* and *Alcea*. Botanists may have thought it a clever combination, since the new *Sidalcea* displayed attributes of both the Virginia Mallow and the Hollyhock. The common names Miniature Hollyhock and Prairie Mallow follow the same logic. The folk names Checkers and Checkerbloom are altogether more original, and may allude to the alternate arrangement of the flowers upon the stem.

Checkerbloom dots grassy hillsides and open forest land in California with its silky, pink flowers. The perennial plants are handsome even while not in flower by virtue of their thin, palm-shaped leaves. Branching spikes from three to four feet tall rise from the foliage in summer. The cup-shaped flowers measure less than two inches across, but crowd the graceful flowering spikes. The colour of the five petals is rosy pink, usually paler in the centre of the blossom around the ivory knob of stamens. Checkerbloom has long been highly regarded in Europe, and careful selection and hybridization has produced flowers of deeper, more subdued tones, as well as more vibrant hues.

Asa Gray was the first to describe the plant sent by one of his western collectors. He presumably gave it the specific name, although he spelled it *malvaeflora*, under which it is still occasionally found. The California native was introduced in 1836 to England.

An adaptable plant, *S. malviflora* performs well in many climates, although it benefits from afternoon shade in warmer regions. It grows well in most soils with regular irrigation. More flowers will often be produced if the stems are removed after the first flush of bloom. It is not always a long-lived perennial, but often perpetuates itself by self-sown seedlings. The stately flowering spikes of Checkerbloom may be stylishly combined with Lady's Mantle, *Alchemilla mollis*, and the diminutive roses—'The Fairy' or 'Bonica'.

Sidalcea malviflora
Malvaceae

Stalks of Checkerbloom, *Sidalcea malviflora*, display the alternate arrangement of flowers on the stems, ABOVE. Coreopsis and Lavender Cotton accent a bowl of Checkerbloom, RIGHT.

Solidago Compositae

134 Wild Flowers

Solidago canadensis CANADA GOLDENROD
Solidago sempervirens SEASIDE GOLDENROD

According to superstition, a stalk of Goldenrod held in hand will reveal hidden treasure. My attempt to find riches about the place revealed not so much as a coin beneath the sofa cushions. Perhaps I will try again, as traditions die hard. Unfortunately, the belief that Goldenrod causes hay fever is still widely held. Although it's been said many times, many ways, this is rubbish.

The pollen of the flowers of the genus *Solidago* is quite heavy, comparatively speaking, and is not wind-borne. The flowers rely instead on insects for fertilization, notably bees and butterflies, and more than a hundred other insects are known to frequent the blossoms. The real culprit during hay fever season is the inconspicuous Ragweed, for whose allergic reactions the brilliant Goldenrod is often blamed. It is possible that highly sensitive individuals may develop sniffles from Goldenrod, just as they may from roses or daisies. The general populace is not at risk.

Native Americans brewed the plentiful blossoms for medicinal tea to treat fevers, cramps, and snakebites. They chewed the flowers for sore throats, and crushed the roots to soothe burns. Early English herbalists valued their native *S. virgaurea* for healing wounds. Turner recommended a leaf tea be given "unto them that are

S. canadensis grows wild near a dairy barn, LEFT. Goldenrod, Bee Balm, artemisia, and clematis vines glow in a summer hearth, RIGHT.

A PORTFOLIO OF ANTIQUE SPECIES 135

wounded within." The genus name is derived from the Latin *solido*, to make whole.

Canada Goldenrod, *S. canadensis*, was introduced to England in 1648 by the younger Tradescant. It is the most widely dispersed Goldenrod, growing plentifully in fields from Newfoundland to Saskatchewan, and in states as far south as Tennessee. Sun-loving Canada Goldenrod has greatly increased since the first settlers arrived in America; heavy timber cutting has created more open fields. A variable perennial species, it normally grows from three to five feet in height and its golden plumes decorate fields and roadsides from August to October.

Seaside Goldenrod, *S. sempervirens*, is a late bloomer native to salty marshes, sand dunes, and rock outcrops along the Atlantic from Nova Scotia to Texas. It is a variable species as well, normally growing from two to eight feet. Seaside Goldenrod is distinguished by its thin, almost succulent leaves that are not notched like those of its Canadian cousin, and by tighter panicles of flowers. The recent discovery of a wild colony growing near John Bartram's historic garden in Philadelphia has led to the speculation that he grew the species—rare in Pennsylvania—and was responsible for its introduction to England.

S. puberula closely resembles *S. sempervirens* and is also called Seaside Goldenrod because it inhabits shorelines along the Atlantic seaboard. It bears yellow flower sprays in late summer and performs admirably in the garden. Many species of *Solidago* are notoriously difficult to identify because the flowers are so similar, but nearly all make gardenworthy subjects.

Goldenrods signal the transformation from summer to autumn in grand style. The plants need no particular attention, and in moist climates, care must be taken that they not overrun the garden. William Robinson warned that they might "exterminate valuable plants." Perhaps he had not heard of the old trick of containing mints and other runners by confining their roots in a bottomless bucket sunk into the earth. This done, the dazzling gold plumes form an effective backdrop for the late blue flowers of *Salvia pitcheri* and Bluebeard, *Caryopteris* × *clandonensis*, as well as the annual Bells of Ireland, *Moluccella laevis*.

European gardeners have long embraced Goldenrods, Robinson notwithstanding, and have developed a number of selections and hybrids. Few American gardeners, Bartram notwithstanding, have been as enthusiastic, perhaps contemptuous of such a plentiful plant, as well as being apprehensive about its undeserved reputation for causing hay fever. This stigma did not follow Goldenrod across the Atlantic. It is used freely for bouquets in the finest restaurants and hotels; the English have indeed discovered the golden treasure.

The blue of the Atlantic underscores the rich hue of Seaside Goldenrod, RIGHT, flowering in late summer.

COMFREY

The ancient Greeks gave *Symphytum* its name, derived from *symphysis*, joining together. The base of the leaf and the stem join or grow together. This in itself is not remarkable, but during the Middle Ages, herbalists took this as a sign of healing properties. The Doctrine of Signatures, which looked for an outer indication—a signature—of a plant's inward virtue, held that *Symphytum officinale* could cause broken bones to grow together. The old folk name Knitbone demonstrates this belief.

The common name Comfrey is taken from the Middle English *cumfierie*, in turn derived from the Latin *conferva*, which also means to knit together. Absolutely everybody in days past agreed on the name, whether in Greek, Latin, or English. *S. officinale* is a native of western Asia and Europe, including Great Britain. Gerard called it Comfrey or Great Consound. For his purposes it was used for much more than knitting bones: the roots, when boiled with sugar, liquorice, coltsfoot, mallow seeds, and poppy seeds, he assured his readers, would cure both aching backs and gonorrhea. Furthermore, the "clammy juyce" of the roots could be drunk with wine to stop the excessive flowing of anything, for it was exceedingly "glutenative." Gerard demonstrated this by instructing that if the juice was poured into a pot where pieces of meat were boiling, they would stick together and become one big "lumpe." It's enough to make one wonder about the fare served at Mrs. Gerard's table.

Colonial women grew Comfrey in their gardens of simples. John Josselyn reported back to England that Compherie, happily, prospered in the New World. It is difficult to imagine a garden where it would not do so. With minimal attention, the perennial plants form a rosette of deep green, hairy leaves up to ten inches in length. Stems rise from three to four feet in height in spring, with the leaves becoming progressively smaller as they ascend the stem.

The flowers are held atop the stems in forked, dangling clusters. The bell-shaped blossoms are a half inch long, and resemble those of the genus *Mertensia*. Coloured pale blue, pink, or white, the flowers bloom heavily in late spring and early summer, and sporadically thereafter. They are frequented by bees. Even after the corolla tubes have fallen, the stamens form an attractive bristly pattern.

Comfrey has escaped into the wild in parts of the northeast United States. Its deep taproots enable the plants to survive periods of low rainfall, though it looks its best in moist soil about which it is not fussy. Although Comfrey is most often grown in herb gardens, the bold leaves and delicate flowers are often valued in perennial borders as a textural contrast to campanulas, daylilies, or candelabra primroses. The variegated form of *S officinale*, its leaves beautifully margined with creamy white, is highly desirable. The hybrid *S.* × *uplandicum* likewise has a variegated form. Comfrey makes a pretty pair with the brassy yellow blossoms of Circle Flower, *Lysimachia punctata*, in partially shaded wild gardens, where there is no danger that they will overwhelm the staunch Comfrey.

Symphytum officinale
Boraginaceae

Comfrey makes a "good for what ails you" tea, ABOVE. Common and variegated *S.* × *uplandicum* thrive with *Ligularia stenocephala* and *Primula sikkimensis*, RIGHT.

Vernonia noveboracensis Compositae

I became acquainted with Ironweed quite by accident. I simply misread a label at a nursery as "Veronica" rather than "Vernonia." I thought I was pretty well versed in my veronicas, so I couldn't pass up what I thought must be a rare species called "noveboracensis." Besides, the thin, narrow leaves of the young plant resembled those of *Veronica longifolia*. Halfway through the summer, as the plant continued to grow lustily, and to heights I had not expected, I decided to check the tag again. I had purchased *Vernonia noveboracensis*, the Ironweed of the Northeast.

The genus was named in honor of William Vernon, an English botanist who collected in Maryland during the late seventeenth century, and Ironweed was first introduced to British horticulturists in 1710. *Vernonia* also includes nearly a thousand species in North and South America as well as Australia. Many of these are tropical trees and shrubs, though the nineteen species in North America are herbaceous perennials.

The genus of *Vernonia* may be likened, in some respects, to a purple counterpart of *Solidago*. Both are tall, vigorous members of Compositae—the tribe of typical daisies, asters, and coneflowers—to which they bear only passing resemblance. The individual small flowers of *V. noveboracensis* are clusters of disc florets without the petals or rays that most daisies possess. They are held in rounded heads on strong stems reaching ten feet in height under ideal conditions; they most often are seen at six feet or so.

Noveboracensis indicates that the plant is of New York, although it is found in moist fields, marshes, and woods from Connecticut to Georgia, west to Ohio and Mississippi. This is one tough plant. A machete or sharp axe is necessary in dividing the strong-as-steel roots of aptly named Ironweed (some might prefer a chainsaw). Juice extracted from the roots was used by Native Americans as a tonic for poor blood, although they had never heard of iron deficiency, and it was not until the advent of television that advertisers made iron-poor blood a national cause for alarm. Ironweed was also used to ease the pain of childbirth and stop bleeding.

Ironweed is among the easiest of plants to grow, if not to position in the garden because of its impressive stature. Clumps are easily established by seed, cutting, but definitely not by division, and thrive in almost any soil in sun or part-sun. Constantly moist soils will promote the most vigorous growth, but Ironweed succeeds well under conditions that suit such companions as Michaelmas Daisy and Purple Coneflower. The lavender tints of the former are especially effective against the violet purple flower heads of Ironweed in the late-blooming border. The rich color is just bold enough to pair with the golden-yellow rudbeckias as well.

IRONWEED

Ironweed prefers a moist site, OPPOSITE. The stems, topped by violet flowers, ABOVE, can reach twelve feet in height but are usually shorter.

A PORTFOLIO OF ANTIQUE SPECIES 141

Hummingbird's Trumpet is among the most charming, and appropriate, of folk names. The bright scarlet tubular flowers of *Zauschneria californica* tempt the little hummers, who often favour red flowers. The one-to-two-inch long flowers are carried in slender sprays above the leaves. The foliage colour is in marked contrast to the flowers, from olive green to silver grey in this variable species. The posture of the plant is variable too; some types grow upright to eighteen inches in height, while others lounge gracefully in spreading mounds. Some selected forms display flowers of creamy white or an exquisite pale peach.

Zauschneria is yet another American plant with a Germanic name, this time commemorating Johann Baptist Zauschner (1737–1799), professor of natural history at the University of Prague. Interestingly, an alternate common name, California Fuchsia, recalls the name of the German Leonhard Fuchs, after which the similar genus *Fuchsia* is named. *Zauschneria*—pronounced something like zowsh-nair-ee-a, accent on the second syllable—is also related to *Oenothera*, *Clarkia*, *Epilobium*, and *Gaura* of the Onagraceae.

Professor Zauschner never saw the flower that bears his name. *Z. californica* was first described in 1831, and was introduced to England in 1847. It has been little grown on either side of the Atlantic since its introduction. Hummingbird's Trumpet inhabits dry, gravelly soil in California and Baja California. Native Americans used its leaves for washing, as well as to treat cuts and sores on themselves and their horses. A medicinal tea was brewed from the flowers for lung and urinary tract problems.

Despite its southwestern origin, *Z. californica* is hardy in many cold-winter areas. So are closely related *Z. arizonica*, which grows in the desert southwest, and *Z. garrettii*, which is found as far north as Idaho. Migrating hummingbirds, moving from Canada to Mexico at the close of the season, have distributed the cold-hardy genes of northern plants ever southward. Thousands of years of this cross-pollination has resulted in a great diversity of zauschnerias; some taxonomists regard all species as one. The plant possesses the ability to withstand cold that defies its natural distribution. It is soundly perennial in my garden in Colorado, for example, where it benefits from relatively dry winters. Sandy, well-drained soil is the key to overwintering Hummingbird's Trumpet elsewhere, such as in England, where it is often grown as a rock plant for sake of better drainage. A sunny location is a prerequisite as well, and *Z. californica* takes no notice whatsoever of baking summer sun even when rainfall is scarce.

Hummingbird's Trumpet blooms in late summer and into the autumn. The scarlet blossoms ignite the late garden palette. The more mounded types are appropriate for rock gardens, where the sprays of flowers tumble gracefully down a slope. The upright types are large enough for a traditional border grouping with Gloriosa Daisies and Blackberry Lily, or in a dryland bed, where the fiery floral display is effective against the silvery stems of artemisias or *Potentilla hippiana*.

Zauschneria Onagraceae

Zauschneria arizonica
HUMMINGBIRD'S TRUMPET

Zauschneria californica
CALIFORNIA FUCHSIA

Z. arizonica spills from a bouquet with agastache and campanula, LEFT. ILLUSTRATION, *Z. californica*. OVERLEAF, *Z. californica* blooms with *Eriogonum umbellatum*.

SOURCES

Anemone canadensis

David Austin; Higher End Nursery; Hoo House Nursery; W E Th Ingwersen.

Anemone × hybrida

Aberconwy Nursery; Broadstone Alpines; Hadspen Garden and Nursery; Kelways Nurseries; Oak Cottage Herb Farm; Old Court Nurseries; Paradise Centre; Rookhope Nurseries; RHS Rosemoor; Sifelle Nursery; Wingwell Nursery.

Anemone sylvestris

Chiltern Seeds; Country Gardens Seeds; David Austin; Eastgrove Cottage Garden Nursery; Glebe Cottage Plants; Paradise Centre; Rookhope Nurseries; Sellet Hall Herbs; Sifelle Nursery; Wingwell Nursery.

Anemone virginiana

B&T World Seeds.

Aquilegia caerulea

Bosvigo Plants; Chiltern Seeds; Country Gardens Seeds; Jack Drake; John Drake; Plants from a Country Garden.

Aquilegia canadensis

Blooms of Bressingham; Chiltern Seeds; Eastgrove Cottage Garden Nursery; Glebe Cottage Plants; W E Th Ingwersen; John Drake; Langthorns Plantery; Stillingfleet Lodge Nurseries.

Aquilegia formosa

B&T World Seeds; Chiltern Seeds; Langthorns Plantery; Netherfield Herbs; Rookhope Nurseries; Sifelle Nursery; Treasures of Tenbury; Unusual Plants; Wingwell Nursery.

Aquilegia vulgaris

B&T World Seeds; Chiltern Seeds; David Austin; Hadspen Garden and Nursery; Hollington Nurseries; Iden Croft Herbs; Netherfield Herbs; Oak Cottage Herb Farm; Polyphant Herb Garden; Rookhope Nurseries.

WHERE TO FIND THE FLOWERS

The addresses for the nurseries noted below are listed alphabetically beginning on page 150.

Armeria maritima

Chiltern Seeds; Country Gardens Seeds; Hillview Hardy Plants; Hollington Nurseries; Iden Croft Herbs; Kingsfield Tree Nursery; Oak Cottage Herb Farm; Paradise Centre; Sellet Hall Herbs; Sifelle Nursery.

Asclepias tuberosa

Blooms of Bressingham; Bridgemere Nurseries; Chiltern Seeds; Country Gardens Seeds; Hollington Nurseries; Langthorns Plantery; Poyntzfield Herb Nursery; Rougham Hall Nurseries.

Aster divaricatus

Widely Available.

Aster novae-angliae

Widely Available.

Aster novi-belgii

Widely Available.

Callirhoe involucrata

Difficult to Find—Ask Your Favourite Supplier to Help.

Chelone obliqua

Blooms of Bressingham; Bridgemere Nurseries; Chiltern Seeds; Country Gardens Seeds; David Austin; Hadspen Garden and Nursery; Holden Clough Nursery; Hopleys Plants; Langthorns Plantery; Perryhill Nurseries; Treasures of Tenbury; Universal Plants; M C Wickenden.

Crysanthemum balsamita

Bridgemere Nurseries; Daphne Ffiske Herbs; Langthorns Plantery; Netherfield Herbs; Polyphant Herb Garden; Poyntzfield Herb Nurseries; Sellet Hall Herbs; Stoke Lacy Herb Gardens.

Chrysanthemum leucanthemum

Blooms of Bressingham; Cheshire Herbs; Eastgrove Cottage Garden Nursery; Kingsfield Tree Nursery; Oak Cottage Herb Farm.

Chrysanthemum parthenium

Cheshire Herbs; Daphne Ffiske Herbs; Hollington Nurseries; Iden Croft Herbs; Netherfield Herbs; Polyphant Herb Garden; Poyntzfield Herb Nurseries; Sellet Hall Herbs; Stoke Lacy Herb Gardens.

Cimicifuga racemosa

Blooms of Bressingham; Clapton Court Gardens; Coton Manor Garden; Kelways Nurseries; Langthorns Plantery; Perryhill Nurseries; Poyntzfield Herb Nursery; Savill Gardens; Treasures of Tenbury; M C Wickenden; Wingwell Nursery.

Coreopsis lanceolata

Bridgemere Nurseries; David Austin; Four Seasons; W E Th Ingwersen; Kelways Nurseries; Plants from a Country Garden; Rookhope Nurseries; Savill Gardens; Treasures of Tenbury; Wintergreen Nurseries.

Coreopsis tinctoria

B&T World Seeds.

Coreopsis verticillata

Charter House Nursery; David Austin; Great Dixter Nurseries; Hadspen Garden and Nursery; Nocutts Nurseries; Plants from a Country Garden; Reginald Kaye; Rushfields of Ledbury; Treasures of Tenbury; Unusual Plants.

Daucus carota

B&T World Seeds; Kingsfield Tree Nursery.

Echinacea purpurea

Charter House Nursery; Chiltern Seeds; Four Seasons; Glebe Cottage Plants; Hadspen Garden and Nursery; Hillview Hardy Plants; Hollington Nurseries; Iden Croft Herbs; Rookhope Nurseries; Sifelle Nursery; Treasures of Tenbury; Unusual Plants.

Epilobium angustifolium

B&T World Seeds; Glebe Cottage Plants; Kingsfield Tree Nursery.

Eupatorium purpureum

Coton Manor Garden; David Austin; Hadspen Garden and Nursery; Hollington Nurseries; Iden Croft Herbs; Netherfield Herbs; Perryhill Nurseries; Poyntzfield Herb Nursery; Rushfields of Ledbury; Unusual Plants.

Eupatorium rugosum

Coton Manor Garden; Four Seasons; Glebe Cottage Plants; Langthorns Plantery; Paradise Centre; Perryhill Nurseries; Plants from a Country Garden; Rougham Hall Nurseries; Treasures of Tenbury; M C Wickenden.

Gaillardia aristata

B&T World Seeds; Glebe Cottage Plants.

Gaillardia pulchella

B&T World Seeds; Chiltern Seeds; Thompson & Morgan.

Gaura lindheimeri

Glebe Cottage Plants; Great Dixter Nurseries; Hadspen Garden and Nursery; Plants from a Country Garden; Rushfields of Ledbury; Unusual Plants; Wintergreen Nurseries.

Gentiana clausa

Difficult to Find—Ask Your Favourite Supplier to Help.

Gillenia trifoliata

Bridgemere Nurseries; Coton Manor Garden; Four Seasons; Great Dixter Nurseries; Langthorns Plantery; Perryhill Nurseries; Poyntzfield Herb Nursery; Reginald Kaye; Treasures of Tenbury; Unusual Plants.

Glaucium flavum

B&T World Seeds; Chiltern Seeds; Glebe Cottage Plants; Stillingfleet Lodge Nurseries.

Helenium autumnale

B&T World Seeds; Chiltern Seeds; Hillview Hardy Plants.

Heuchera americana

Foliage and Unusual Plants; Four Seasons; Unusual Plants.

Heuchera sanguinea

Bridgemere Nurseries; Foliage and Unusual Plants; Glebe Cottage Plants; Hillview Hardy Plants; Holden Clough Nursery; Oak Cottage Herb Farm; Treasures of Tenbury; Wingwell Nursery.

Ipomopsis aggregata

B&T World Seeds.

Ipomopsis rubra

Difficult to Find—Ask Your Favourite Supplier to Help.

Lathyrus latifolius

Widely Available.

Liatris pycnostachya

B&T World Seeds; Chiltern Seeds; Hillview Hardy Plants; Plants from a Country Garden; Wintergreen Nurseries.

Liatris spicata

Charter House Nursery; Four Seasons; Hollington Nurseries; Iden Croft Herbs; Langthorns Plantery; Rookhope Nurseries; Rushfields of Ledbury; Treasures of Tenbury; Unusual Plants.

Lilium canadense

B&T World Seeds; Jacques Amand.

Lilium philadelphicum

B&T World Seeds; Chiltern Seeds; Jacques Amand.

Lilium superbum

B&T World Seeds; Jacques Amand.

Lilium tigrinum

Michael Jefferson-Brown; Plaxtol Nurseries; Rupert Bowlby.

Lobelia cardinalis

Widely Available.

Lobelia siphilitica

Widely Available.

Mentzelia laevicaulis

B&T World Seeds.

Mentzelia lindleyi

B&T World Seeds; Chiltern Seeds; Thompson & Morgan.

Monarda citriodora

B&T World Seeds; Hollington Nurseries; Iden Croft Herbs; Poyntzfield Herb Nursery.

Monarda didyma

B&T World Seeds; Daphne Ffiske Herbs; Hadspen Garden And Nursery; Iden Croft Herbs; Oak Cottage Herb Farm; Poyntzfield Herb Nursery; Stoke Lacy Herb Gardens.

Monarda punctata

B&T World Seeds; Langthorns Plantery.

Oenothera biennis

Chiltern Seeds; Iden Croft Herbs; Netherfield Herbs; Oak Cottage Herb Farm; Polyphant Herb Garden; Poyntzfield Herb Nursery; Sellet Hall Herbs.

Oenothera caespitosa

Chiltern Seeds; Old Court Nurseries.

Oenothera fruticosa

B&T World Seeds.

Oenothera speciosa

B&T World Seeds; Chiltern Seeds; Hopleys Plants; Plants From A Country Garden.

Papaver nudicaule

B&T World Seeds; Langthorns Plantery.

Papaver rhoeas

B&T World Seeds; Chiltern Seeds; Hollington Nurseries; Iden Croft Herbs; Poyntzfield Herb Nursery.

Penstemon barbatus

Blooms of Bressingham; Coton Manor Garden; David Austin; Glebe Cottage Plants; Kelways Nurseries; Langthorns Plantery; Perryhill Nurseries; Rougham Hall Nurseries; Unusual Plants; Wingwell Nursery.

Penstemon pinifolius

Widely Available.

Penstemon strictus

Green Farm Plants; Sussex Country Gardens; M C Wickenden.

Physostegia formosior

Difficult to Find—Ask Your Favourite Supplier to Help.

Physostegia virginiana

B&T World Seeds.

Ratibida columnifera

B&T World Seeds; Tim Ingram.

Rudbeckia hirta

B&T World Seeds; Chiltern Seeds; Thompson & Morgan.

Rudbeckia laciniata

B&T World Seeds; Langthorns Plantery; Stillingfleet Lodge Nurseries.

Rudbeckia triloba

B&T World Seeds.

Saponaria officinalis

Chiltern Seeds; Daphne Ffiske Herbs; David Austin; Hadspen Garden and Nursery; Hollington Nurseries; Iden Croft Herbs; Kingsfield Tree Nursery; Netherfield Herbs; Oak Cottage Herb Farm; Plants from a Country Garden; Polyphant Herb Garden; Stoke Lacy Herb Gardens.

Sidalcea malviflora

Plants from a Country Garden; M C Wickenden; Wintergreen Nurseries.

Solidago canadensis

B&T World Seeds; Chiltern Seeds; Langthorns Plantery; Thompson & Morgan.

Solidago sempervirens

Difficult to Find—Ask Your Favourite Supplier to Help.

Symphytum officinale

Bridgemere Nurseries; Daphne Ffiske Herbs; Holden Clough Nursery; Hollington Nurseries; Iden Croft Herbs; Oak Cottage Herb Farm; Polyphant Herb Gardens; Poyntzfield Herb Nursery; Stoke Lacy Herb Gardens.

Vernonia noveboracensis

Difficult to Find—Ask Your Favourite Supplier to Help.

Zauschneria arizonica

Hopleys Plants.

Zauschneria californica

B&T World Seeds; Chiltern Seeds; M C Wickenden.

Nurseries and Seed Merchants

Aberconwy Nursery
Graig
Glan Conwy, Colwyn Bay
Clwydd LL28 7TL

B&T World Seeds
Whitnell House
Fiddington, Bridgwater
Somerset TA5 1JE

Blooms of Bressingham
Diss
Norfolk IP22 2AB

Bosvigo Plants
Bosvigo Lane
Truro
Cornwall TR1 3NH

Bregover Plants
Hillbrooke, Middlewood
North Hill, Launceston
Cornwall PL15 7NN

Bridgemere Nurseries
Bridgemere
nr. Nantwich
Cheshire CW5 7QB

Broadstone Alpines
13 The Nursery
High Street, Sutton Courtnay
Abingdon
Oxfordshire OX14 4UA

Charter House Nursery
Charter House, Troqueer Road
Dumfriesshire DG2 7RE

Cheshire Herbs
Fourfields
Forest Road, Little Budworth
Cheshire CW6 9ES

Chiltern Seeds
Bortree Stile
Ulverston
Cumbria LA12 7PB

Clapton Court Gardens
Crewkerne
Somerset TA18 8PT

Coton Manor Garden
nr. Guilsborough
Northampton NN6 8RQ

Country Gardens Seeds
60 Wickham Road
Shirley, Croydon
Surrey CR9 8AG

David Austin
Bowling Green Lane
Albrighton
Wolverhampton WV7 3HB

Daphne Ffiske Herbs
Rosemary Cottage
Bramerton, Norwich
Norfolk NR14 7DW

Eastgrove Cottage Garden Nursery
Sankyns Green
nr. Shrawley, Little Witley
Worcestershire WR6 6LQ

Foliage and Unusual Plants
The Dingle, Pilsgate
Stamford
Lincoln PE9 3HW

Four Seasons
Forncett St. Mary
Norwich
Norfolk NR16 1JT

Glebe Cottage Plants
Pixie Lane
Warkleigh, Umberleigh
Devon EX3 9DH

Great Dixter Nurseries
Northiam, Rye
East Sussex TN31 6PH

Green Farm Plants
Bentley
Farnham
Surrey GU10 5JX

HADSPEN GARDEN AND NURSERY
Castle Cary
Somerset BA7 7NG

HIGHER END NURSERY
Hale, Fordingbridge
Hampshire SP6 2RA

HILLVIEW HARDY PLANTS
Worfield
nr. Bridgenorth
Shropshire WV15 5NT

HOLDEN CLOUGH NURSERY
Holden
Bolton-by-Bowland
Clitheroe, Lancashire BB7 4PF

HOLLINGTON NURSERIES
Woolton Hill
Newbury
Berkshire RG15 9XT

HOO HOUSE NURSERY
Hoo House, Gloucester Road
Tewkesbury
Gloucester GL20 7DA

HOPLEYS PLANTS
High Street
Much Hadham
Hertfordshire SG10 6BU

IDEN CROFT HERBS
Frittenden Road
Staplehurst
Kent TN12 0DH

W E TH INGWERSEN
Birch Farm Nursery
Gravetye, East Grinstead
West Sussex RH19 4LE

JACQUES AMAND
The Nurseries
Clamp Hill, Stanmore
Middlesex HA7 3JS

JACK DRAKE
Inshriach Alpine Nursery
Aviemore
Inverness PH22 1QS

JOHN DRAKE
Hardwicke House
Fen Ditton
Cambridge CB5 8TF

KELWAYS NURSERIES
Langport
Somerset TA10 9SL

KINGSFIELD TREE NURSERY
Broadenham Lane, Winsham
Chard, Somerset TA20 4JF

LANGTHORNS PLANTERY
High Cross Lane West
Little Canfield, Dunmow
Essex CM6 1TD

MICHAEL JEFFERSON-BROWN
Broadgate, Weston Hills
Spalding, Lincolnshire PE12 6DQ

NETHERFIELD HERBS
Nether Street, Rougham
nr. Bury St. Edmunds
Suffolk IP30 9LW

NOTCUTTS NURSERIES
Woodbridge
Suffolk IP12 4AF

OAK COTTAGE HERB FARM
Nesscliffe
nr. Shrewsbury
Shropshire SY4 1DB

OLD COURT NURSERIES
Colwell
nr. Malvern
Worcestershire WR13 6QE

PARADISE CENTRE
Twinstead Road
Lamarsh, Bures
Suffolk CO8 5EX

PERRYHILL NURSERIES
Hartfield
Sussex TN7 4JP

PLANTS FROM A COUNTRY GARDEN
The Thatched Cottage
Duck Lane, Ludgershall
Aylesbury, Bucks HP18 9NZ

PLAXTOL NURSERIES
The Spoute, Plaxtol
Sevenoaks, Kent TN15 0QR

POLYPHANT HERB GARDEN
Polyphant, Launceston
Cornwall PL15 7PS

POYNTZFIELD HERB NURSERY
Black Isle, Dingwell
Ross and Cromarty IV7 8LX

RHS ROSEMOOR
Royal Horticultural Society
Rosemoor
Great Torrington
Devon EX38 8PH

REGINALD KAYE
Waithman Nurseries
Silverdale, Carnforth
Lancashire LA5 0TY

ROOKHOPE NURSERIES
Rookhope
Upper Weardale
Durham DL13 2DD

ROUGHAM HALL NURSERIES
Ipswich Road, Rougham
Bury St. Edmunds
Suffolk IP30 9LZ

RUPERT BOWLBY
Gatton, Reigate
Surrey RH2 0TA

RUSHFIELDS OF LEDBURY
Ross Road, Ledbury
Hereford HR8 2LP

SAVILL GARDENS
Crown Estate Office
The Great Park, Windsor
Berkshire SL4 2HT

SELLET HALL HERBS
Whittington, via Carnforth
Lancashire LA6 2QF

SIFELLE NURSERY
The Walled Garden
Newick Park
Newick, Sussex

STILLINGFLEET LODGE NURSERIES
Stillingfleet
Yorkshire YO4 6HW

STOKE LACY HERB GARDENS
Bromyard
Hereford HR7 4JH

TABLE OF CONVERSIONS

Measurements are given in imperial units throughout the book. Please refer to this chart to find the metric equivalent.

1 inch = 2.54 centimetres
1 foot = 30.48 centimetres
1 foot 6 inches (1½ feet) = 45.72 centimetres
2 feet = 60.96 centimetres
3 feet (1 yard) = 91.44 centimetres
10 feet = 3.05 metres

SUSSEX COUNTRY GARDENS
Newhaven Road
Kingston, nr. Lewes
East Sussex
BN7 3NE

THOMPSON & MORGAN
London Road, Ipswich
Suffolk IP2 0BA

TIM INGRAM
Ashford Road
Faversham, Kent ME13 8XW

TREASURES OF TENBURY
Burford House Gardens
Tenbury Wells
Worcestershire WR15 8HQ

UNUSUAL PLANTS
Beth Chatto Gardens
Elmstead Market, Colchester
Essex CO7 7DB

M C WICKENDEN
Cally Gardens, Gatehouse of Fleet
Castle Douglas
Scotland DG7 2DJ

WINGWELL NURSERY
Top Street
Wing, Oakham
Leicestershire LE15 8SE

WINTERGREEN NURSERIES
Bringsty Common
Worcester WR6 5UW

154 Wild Flowers

BIBLIOGRAPHY

Anderson, Berta. *Wild Flower Name Tales*. Colorado Springs: Century One Press, 1976.

Armitage, Ethel. *A Country Garden*. New York: The Macmillan Company, 1936.

Birchfield, Emerson R. "The Negligent Gardener." *Green Thumb News* (February 1988): 5.

Bonta, Marcia. "John Bartram and His Garden." *American Horticulturist* (December 1985): 24–29.

Bubel, Nancy. "Goldenrods for the Garden?" *Horticulture* (August 1984): 20–23.

Charlesworth, Geoffrey. "Plant Goals." *Bulletin of the American Rock Garden Society* (Summer 1990): 187–192.

Choukas-Bradley, Melanie, and Polly Alexander. *City of Trees*. Washington, D.C.: Acropolis Books, 1981.

Clark, Elizabeth Cernota. "Gaura." *Horticulture* (June 1990): 80.

Coats, Alice M. *Flowers and their Histories*. London: Hulton Press, 1956.

Colden, Jane. *Botanic Manuscript of Jane Colden*. New York: Chanticleer Press, 1963.

Coombes, Allen J. *Collingridge Dictionary of Plant Names*. London: Newnes, 1985.

Crockett, James Underwood. *Wildflower Gardening*. Alexandria, Va.: Time-Life Books, 1971.

Dupree, A. Hunter. *Asa Gray*. Cambridge, Mass: The Belknap Press of Harvard University Press, 1968.

Earle, Alice Morse. *Old Time Gardens*. New York: The Macmillan Co., 1901.

Ewan, Joseph. *Rocky Mountain Naturalists*. Denver: The University of Denver Press, 1950.

Ewan, Joseph, ed. *A Short History of Botany in the United States*. New York: Hafner Publishing Company, 1969.

Everett, Thomas H. *The New York Botanical Garden Illustrated Encyclopedia of Horticulture*. New York: Garland Publishing, 1981.

Feltwell, John. *The Naturalist's Garden*. Topsfield, Mass.: Salem House Publishers, 1987.

Ferguson, Mary, and Saunders, Richard. *Wildflowers*. Toronto: Van Nostrand Reinhold, 1976.

Foster, Steven. "Echinaceas." *American Horticulturist* (August 1985): 14.

Foster, Steven, and Duke, James A. *A Field Guide to Medicinal Plants*. Boston: Houghton Mifflin, 1990.

Goode, Jeanne. "Wild Lace." *Horticulture* (August 1985): 15–16.

Harmon, Stanley M. "Liatris." *American Horticulturist* (June 1987): 25.

Harvard University. *Gray Herbarium Index*. Boston: G. K. Hall, 1968.

Henderson, Peter. *Henderson's Handbook of Plants*. New York: Peter Henderson, 1890.

Houk, Rose. *Wildflowers of the American West*. San Francisco: Chronicle Books, 1987.

Index kewensis. Oxford: Oxford University Press, 1895.

Jekyll, Gertrude. *Colour Schemes for the Flower Garden*. London: Country Life, 1908.

Jekyll, Gertrude. *Wood and Garden*. London: Longmans, Green, 1899.

Johnson, Lady Bird, and Carlton B. Lees. *Wildflowers Across America*. New York: Abbeville Press, 1988.

Kelaidis, Panayoti. "Tethyan Plants." *Mountain, Plain, and Garden* (Fall 1990): 8–13.

Lacy, Allen. "Confessions of a Magpie Gardener." *Garden Design* (Summer 1985): 108.

Leighton, Ann. *Early American Gardens "for Meate or Medicine."* Boston: Houghton Mifflin, 1970.

Lloyd, Christopher. *The Well-Chosen Garden*. London: Hamish Hamilton, 1984.

Mabey, Richard, and Tony Evans. *The Flowering of Britain*. London: Chatto and Windus, 1989.

Nehrling, Arno, and Irene Nehrling. *The Picture Book of Annuals*. New York: Hearthside Press, 1966.

Polunin, Oleg. *Collins Photoguide to Wild Flowers of Britain and Northern Europe*. London: William Collins, 1988.

Quinn, Vernon. *Roots, Their Place in Life and Legend*. New York: Frederick A. Stokes, 1938.

The Reader's Digest Association Limited. *Wild Flowers of Britain*. London: The Reader's Digest Association, 1981.

Rickett, Harold W. *Wild Flowers of the United States*. 6 vols. New York: McGraw-Hill, 1966–1976.

Robinson, William. *The English Flower Garden*. London: John Murray, 1883.

Rodgers, Andrew Denny III. *American Botany 1873–1892*. Princeton: Princeton University Press, 1944.

Sawyers, Claire E., ed. *Gardening With Wildflowers and Native Plants*. New York: Brooklyn Botanic Garden, 1989.

Singleton, Esther. *The Shakespeare Garden*. New York: The Century Co., 1922.

Skinner, Charles M. *Myths and Legends of Flowers, Trees, Fruits, and Plants*. Philadelphia: J. B. Lippincott, 1911.

Swain, Roger B. "Palms and Parrots." *Horticulture* (July 1988): 49–55.

Taylor, Julia. *Collecting Garden Plants*. London: J. M. Dent, 1988.

Thomas, Graham Stuart. *Perennial Garden Plants or The Modern Florilegium*. London: J. M. Dent, 1982.

Waters, Michael. *The Garden in Victorian Literature*. Aldershot: Scholar Press, 1988.

INDEX

Page numbers in italic indicate illustrations

A

Acidanthera bicolor, 78
Aegopodium podagraria (Bishop's Weed), 35
agastache, *142*
Alchemilla mollis (Lady's Mantle), *8*, 132
alliums, *130*
Alum Root, 96, 97
anemones, 12, 13, *54*, 55
    Anemone canadensis (Canadian Anemone), 55
    Anemone coronaria, 55
    Anemone hupehensis, 55
    Anemone sylvestris (Snowdrop Windflower), 55
    Anemone virginiana (Thimbleweed), *54*, 55
    Anemone vitifolia, 55
    Anemone × hybrida (Japanese Windflower), 55, *81*, 123
Apple-blossom Grass, *86–87*
Aquilegia caerulea (Rocky Mountain Columbine), *56*, 57
Aquilegia canadensis (Canadian Columbine), 25, *26*, 57
Aquilegia formosa (Jester's Cap), *19*, 57
Aquilegia vulgaris (Granny bonnets), 57
Armeria maritima (Sea Pink), *58–59*
Armitage, Ethel, 33, 36
Artemisia, *42–43*, 78, 96, *122*, *135*, 143
Asclepias tuberosa (Butterfly Weed), *60–61*
Aster divaricatus (White Wood Aster), *17*, 63
Aster novae-angliae (Michaelmas Daisy), *62*, 63
Aster novi-belgii (New York Aster), *62*, 63
A-thousand-charms, 69, 70, *71*
azaleas, 43
Aztecs, 22–23

B

Babylon, Hanging Gardens of, 22
Bachelor's Buttons, *18*, 36, 38, *116*
Balloon Flower, 24
Banister, John, 78
Barton, Benjamin Smith, 28, 29, 110
Bartram, John, 26, 73, 107, 114, 136
Bartram, William, 26
Bee Balm, *112–13*, 114, *135*
Bells of Ireland, 136
Bishop's Weed, 35
Bitterroot, 30
Black Snakeroot, *72*, 73
Black-eyed Susan, 45–46, *105*, *122*, 127, *128–29*
Blazing Star, 47, *110–11*
Bleeding Heart, 24
Bluebeard, 136
Bluebells, 16, 109
Bluebonnets, 16
Bluebottle, 36
Bougainvillea, 16
Bowman's Root, *90–91*
Bradbury, John, 124
Breck, Joseph, 87
Bridges, Robert, 93
Brodiaea laxa, 30
Brooks, Nathaniel, 25
Brown-eyed Susan, *45*, *62*, *126–27*, *128*
Bugbane, *72*, 73
Burnett, 56
Buttercup, 26, 55
Butterfly Weed, *60–61*
Button Snakeroot, 103, *104–5*

C

cactus, *121*
Calendula officinalis (Pot Marigold), 25
California Fuchsia, 143, *144*
California Poppy, *18*, *30*
California Star, *110*
Calliopsis, *31*, 75
Callirhoe involucrata (Wine Cup), *64–65*
Campanula, 57, 80, *142*
Canada Goldenrod, *134*, 136
Canadian Anemone, 55
Canadian Columbine, 25, *26*, 27
Cardinal Flower, 24–25, 88, *108*, 109
Castilleja, 44
Catanache caerulea (Cupid's Dart), 66
Cather, Willa, 85
Centaurea cyanus (Cornflower), 36, 78, *116*
Centranthus ruber (Jupiter's Beard), 34
Chamomile, 34
Chatto, Beth, 87
Chaucer, Geoffrey, 23, 57
Checkerbloom, *132–33*
Chelone obliqua (Turtle-head), 66, 67
Chicory, *35*
Chrysanthemum balsamita (Costmary), 69, 70
Chrysanthemum leucanthemum (Ox-eye Daisy), *18*, 26, 69, 70, *71*
Chrysanthemum parthenium (Feverfew), *68*, 69, 70
Cichorium intybus (Chicory), *35*
Cimicifuga racemosa (Black Snakeroot), *72*, 73
Clark, William, 29–30
Clarkia, *8*
Clematis, *90–91*, *135*
Closed Gentian, *88–89*
Colden, Jane, 26, 60, 67, 107, 114, 128
Cole, William, 11
Collinson, Peter, 26, 73, 107, 114
Columbine, *19*, 25, 26, *56*, 57
Comfrey, 138, *139*
Compton, Henry, 78
Coralbells, *18*, 96
Coreopsis, *133*
    Coreopsis grandiflora, 74
    Coreopsis lanceolata (Tickseed), *74*, 75
    Coreopsis tinctoria (Calliopsis), 75
    Coreopsis verticillata (Thread-Leaf Coreopsis), *74–75*
corn, 25
Corn Cockle, 36
Cornflower, 36, *116*
Coronado, Francisco Vasques de, 34, 36
Costmary, 69, 70
Coulter's Botanical Gazette, 120
Cow Parsnip, *14*, 80
Culpeper, Nicholas, 55
Cupid's Dart, 66, *86*

D

Daisies, *18*, 23, 26, *69–71*, *102–4*, *126–29*, *140–41*
Dandelions, 34, 36
Darwin, Charles, 120
Daucus carota (Queen Anne's Lace), 76, 77, *130*
Deane, Sir Drew, 25
Denver Botanic Garden, *102*
Doctrine of Signatures, 138
Downing, Andrew Jackson, 42
Drummond, Thomas, 65

E

Earle, Maria Theresa, 96
Easter Flower, 69, 70, *71*
Echinacea purpurea (Purple Coneflower), 78, *79*, *105*, *121*
Echinocystis lobata (Mock Cucumber), *26*
Elecampane, 34, *54*
Engelmann, George, 96
Epilobium angustifolium (Willow Herb), *13*, *80–81*
Eriogonum umbellatum, 44, *144*
Eupatorium purpureum (Joe Pye Weed), *43*, 45, *82–83*, 88
Eupatorium rugosum (White Snakeroot), 83
Evening Primrose, 77, *116–17*
Everlasting Pea, *15*, *100–101*

F

False Dragon Head, *123*
Feverfew, 34, *56*, 68, 69, 70
Firewheel, *31*, *84*, 85
Fish, Margery, 49
Flanders Poppy, 118, *119*
flax, *51*
Fleabane, *61*
Fleur-de-lis, 34
Fortune, Robert, 55
Franklin, Benjamin, 26
Fremont, John, 30
Fuchs, Leonard, 143

G

Gaillard de Charentonneau, M., 85
Gaillardia aristata (Firewheel), *31*, *84*, 85
Gaillardia pulchella (Indian Blanket), 47, *85*
Gaillardia × *grandiflora*, 85
Garden Phlox, *78*
Gaura lindheimeri (Apple-blossom Grass), *86–87*
Gayfeather, 47, *102*, 103, 105
Genista tinctoria (Yellow broom), 34
Gentiana clausa (Closed Gentian), *88–89*
Gerard, John, 23, 25, 34, 53, 55, 69, 77, 101, 109, 131, 138
Gillen, Arnold, 90
Gillenia trifoliata (Bowman's Root), *90–91*
Glaucium flavum (Horned Poppy), *92*, 93
Gloriosa Daisies, 128, *143*
Goldenrod, 42, 77, *134–37*
Granny Bonnets, 57
Gray, Asa, 28–29, 30–31, 62, 87, 96, 110, 120, 132
Great Lobelia, *29*, 109
Greene, Alfred, 120
Greene, Edward, 31
Green-headed Coneflower, *128*
Gunnison, John, 30

H

Hanbury, William, 114, 128
Harebell, *61*
Hattie's Pincushion, *59*
Hawthorne, Nathaniel, 21
Helenium autumnale (Sneezeweed), *94–95*, *126–27*
Helianthus tuberosus (Jerusalem Artichoke), 25, 29
Hemerocallis fulva (Tawny Daylily), 36
Henderson, Peter, 67, 99, 110, 127
Heracleum sphondylium (Cow Parsnip), *14*, 80
Hermann, Franz, 62
Heuchera americana (Alum Root), 96, *97*
Heuchera sanguinea (Coralbells), *18*, 96
Hey, Rebecca, 116
Hibberd, Shirley, 101
Hill, John, 81
Horned Poppy, *92*, 93
Horsemint, *114*
Hummingbird's Trumpet, *142*, 143

I

Iceland Poppy, *118*
Impatiens capensis (Jewel Weed), *46*
Incas, 23
Indian Blanket, 47, *85*
Indian Paintbrushes, *44*
Indians. *See* Native Americans
Indian Tobacco, 109
Ipomopsis rubra (Standing Cypress), *98*, 99
Iris pallida, 96
Iris pseudoacorus (Fleur-de-lis), 34
Ironweed, *45*, *140–41*

J

James, Edwin, 57
Japanese Windflower, 55, 81, 123
Jefferson, Thomas, 29, 31
Jekyll, Gertrude, 44, 49, 62, 96, 131
Jerusalem Artichoke, 25, 29
Jester's Cap, 57
Jewel Weed, *46*
Joe Pye Weed, *43*, 45, *82–83*, 88
Josselyn, John, 26, 69, 138
Jupiter's Beard, 34

K

Keats, John, 116
Kerr, William, 107
Kudzu Vine, 36

L

Lacy, Allen, 49
Ladies' Cushions, 58
Ladyslipper Orchids, 44
Lamb's Ears, 59, 65, 96
Larkspur, *78*
Lathyrus latifolius (Everlasting Pea), *15*, *100–101*
Lavender Cotton, 65, *133*
l'Obel, Matthias de, 109
Lemon Mint, 114, *115*
Le Nôtre, André, 24
Lewis and Clark expedition, 29–30, 85

Liatris pycnostachya (Button Snakeroot), 103, *104–5*
Liatris spicata (Gayfeather), 47, *102*, 103, 105
Ligularia stenocephala, 139
lilies, 23, 107
    Lilium canadense (Meadow Lily), 26, 107
    Lilium candidum (Madonna Lily), 14, *15*, 107
    Lilium martagon, 107
    Lilium michauxii, 107
    Lilium philadelphicum (Wood Lily), 107
    Lilium superbum (Turk's-cap Lily), *106–7*
    Lilium tigrinum (Tiger Lily), 107
Lily of the Valley, 34
Lindheimer, Ferdinand, 87
Lindley, John, 110
Linnaeus, Carolus, 14, 26, 78, 99, 109, 127
Lloyd, Christopher, 49
lobelia, 109
    Lobelia cardinalis (Cardinal Flower), *24–25*, 88, *108*, 109
    Lobelia inflata (Indian Tobacco), 109
    Lobelia siphilitica (Great Lobelia), *29*, 109
Long, Stephen, 30, 57
Loudon, Jane, 109
Lupines, *23*
Lychnis flos-cuculi (Ragged Robin), *14*, 34
Lythrum salicaria (Purple Loosestrife), 36, *37*

M

Macleaya cordata (Plume Poppy), 95, *121*
Madonna Lily, 14, *15*, 107
Martagon Lily, 34
Matted Evening Primrose, *117*
Maund, Benjamin, 75
Meadow Lily, 26, 107
Meadow Pearl, 69, 70, *71*
Mealycup Sage, *86*
Measure-of-love, 69, 70, *71*
Mentzel, Christian, 110
Mentzelia laevicaulis (Blazing Star), 47, *110–11*
Mentzelia lindleyi (California Star), 110
Mexican Hat, *124–25*
Michaelmas Daisy, *62*, 63, 141
Michaux, André, 28, 105, 107
Mimulus cardinalis, 105
mint, *112–15*

Mock Cucumber, *26*
Monarda citriodora (Lemon Mint), 114, *115*
Monarda didyma (Bee Balm), *112–13*, 114, 135
Monarda punctata (Horsemint), *114*
Monardes, Nicholas, 114
mullein, 12

N

narcissus, 12
nasturtiums, 22
Native Americans, 12, 22–23, 26, 30, 34, 55, 60, 65, 73, 75, 78, *81*, 83, 95, 109, 110, 114, 127–28, 135, 141, 143
Nebuchadnezzar, King, 22
New England Aster, 46
New York Aster, *62*, 63
Nuttall, Thomas, 28–29, 65, 75, 117, 124

O

Obedience, 81, *122*, 123
Oenothera biennis (Evening Primrose), *116*, 117
Oenothera caespitosa (Matted Evening Primrose), *117*
Oenothera fruticosa (Sundrop), 116, *117*
Oenothera speciosa (White Evening Primrose), *117*
Old Gooseneck, 54, *81*
Ox-eye Daisy, *18*, *26*, 69, 70, *71*

P

pansies, 25
Parkinson, John, 23, 58, 69, 100, 109, 128, 131
Parry, Charles, 31
Partridge Feathers, *59*, 96
Pearly Everlasting, 25, *61*, 95
penstemons, *112*, 120, 131
    Penstemon barbatus (Scarlet Bugler), 120, *121*
    Penstemon pinifolius (Prairie Fire), 120
    Penstemon strictus (Rocky Mountain Penstemon), 120
Phlox paniculata, 122
Physostegia formosior (False Dragon Head), *123*
Physostegia virginiana (Obedience), 81, *122*, 123
Pike, Zebulon, 30
Pinks, 24, 25, 45, *58–59*
Pitcher Plant, 26
Pliny the Elder, 58, 77
Pliny the Younger, 22
Plume Poppy, 95, *121*
Plutarch, 69

poppies, 23, *51*, 118
    Papaver nudicaule (Iceland Poppy), *118*
    Papaver radicatum, 118
    Papaver rhoeas (Flanders Poppy), 118, *119*
    Plume Poppy, 95, *121*
    Shirley Poppy, 118
Pot Marigold, 25
Prairie Fire, *120*
primroses, 13, 23, *116–17*, *139*
Primula sikkimensis, *139*
Pueraria lobata (Kudzu Vine), 36
Puncture Vine, 18, 34
Purple Coneflower, 78, *79*, *105*, *121*, 124, 141
Purple Loosestrife, 36, *37*
Pursh, Frederick, 124

Q

Queen Anne's Lace, *76*, 77, *130*

R

Ragged Robin, *14*, 34
Ragweed, 135
Ratibida columnifera (Mexican Hat), *124–25*
Redouté, Jean-Pierre, 28
rhododendrons, 43
Robinson, William, 44, 60, 90
Rocky Mountain Columbine, *56*, 57
Rocky Mountain Garland, 30
Rocky Mountain Penstemon, 120
Rosa rugosa, 34
Rosemary, 14, 25
roses, 16, 22, 25, 34, 90
Rudbeck, Olaf, 127
rudbeckias, *42–43*, 141
    Rudbeckia hirta (Black-eyed Susan), 45–46, *105*, *122*, 127, *128–29*
    Rudbeckia laciniata (Green-headed Coneflower), *128*
    Rudbeckia triloba (Brown-eyed Susan), 45, 62, *126–27*, 128
Rue, 13, *15*
Ruskin, John, 118

S

Sacajawea, 30
Sackville-West, Vita, 49
St. Augustine, 49
St.-John's-wort, 14, 34
salvias, 87, 96, 136
   Salvia officinalis (sage), 13, *96*
   Salvia sclarea, 79
Santolina chamaecyparissus (Lavender Cotton), 65, *133*
Saponaria officinalis (Soapwort), 34, *130–31*
Scarlet Bugler, 120, *121*
Scribner, F. Lamson, 41
Sea Holly, 93
Sea Lavender, *86*
Sea Pink, 45, *58–59*
Seaside Goldenrod, 136, *137*
Sedum spectabile, *29*, 96
Shakespeare, William, 57
Shirley Poppy, 118
Sidalcea malviflora (Checkerbloom), *132–33*
Skunk Cabbage, 26
Skyrocket, *99*
Sneezeweed, *94–95*, *126–27*
Snowdrop Windflower, 55
Soapwort, 34, *130–31*
Solidago canadensis (Canada Goldenrod), *134*, 136
Solidago puberula, 136
Solidago sempervirens (Seaside Goldenrod), 136, *137*
Solidago virgaurea, 135
Spiderwort, 42
Stachys byzantina (Lamb's Ears), 59, 65, 96
Standing Cypress, *98*, 99
Star of Bethlehem, 14, *16*
statice, 58
Sundrop, 116, *117*
Sunflowers, 16, 23
Sutherland, William, 62
Sweet Pea, 101
Symphytum officinale (Comfrey), 138, *139*
Symphytum × *uplandicum*, 138, *139*

T

Tanacetum vulgare (Tansy), *38–39*
tarragon, 25
Tawny Daylily, 36
Theobroma cacao (chocolate), 23
Thimbleweed, *54*, 55
Thomas, Graham Stuart, 85, 95
Thread-Leaf Coreopsis, *74–75*
thyme, 25, 114
Tickseed, *74*, 75
Tiger Lily, 107
Torrey, John, 30–31, 87, 110
Tradescant, John, 42, 57, 109, 128, 136
Trembling Star, *69*, *70*, *71*
Tumbleweed, 36
Turk's-cap Lily, *106–7*
Turner, William, 23, 55, 135–36
Turtle-head, 47, *66–67*, 88
Twalmey, Loisa Anne, 57

V

Vernon, William, 141
Vernonia noveboracensis (Ironweed), 45, *140–41*
Veronica, 14, 141
violets, 13, 23, 25, 29
von Heucher, Johann Heinrich, 96

W

Wallflower, *15*
White Evening Primrose, *117*
White Snakeroot, 83
Whiteweed, *69*, *70*, *71*
White Wood Aster, *17*, *63*
wild ginger, 26
wild wheat, 34
Wilks, William, 118
Willow Herb, *13*, *80–81*
windflowers, 55
Wine Cup, *64–65*
Winthrop, John, 25
Wislizenus, Adolph, 96
Witches Blood, 34
Wood, William, 26
Wood Lily, *107*
Wormwood, *122*

X

Xochimilco, 22

Y

Yarrow, 34
Yellow broom, 34
Yellow Gentian, 88
Yellow loosestrife, 13
Yellow primrose, 16
yucca, 44

Z

Zauschner, Johann Baptist, 143
Zauschneria arizonica (Hummingbird's Trumpet), *142*, 143
Zauschneria californica (California Fuchsia), 143, *144*
Zea mays (corn), 25
Zinnia grandiflora, 22, *28*, *29*, 87, 99
Zuni Indians, 34